SLAVE IMPORTATION AFFIDAVIT REGISTERS FOR NINE GEORGIA COUNTIES, 1818 – 1847

SLAVE IMPORTATION AFFIDAVIT REGISTERS FOR NINE GEORGIA COUNTIES, 1818 - 1847

Dawn Watson

Bone Diggers Press, Clayton, GA
www.bonediggerspress.com

In Memoriam
Andrea Burrell Potts
1953 – 2005

Published by Bone Diggers Press, P. O. Box 1049, Clayton, GA, 30525.

Printed by CreateSpace (www.createspace.com).

ISBN-10: 0-615-73541-X
ISBN-13: 978-0-615-73541-2

Please direct questions to the publisher or the author:
Dawn Watson
P. O. Box 292
Rabun Gap, GA 30568
www.dncresearchgroup.com

Also available from this author:
Rabun County, Georgia, Newspapers, 1894 - 1899

TABLE OF CONTENTS

LIST OF ILLUSTRATIONS

PREFACE

This compilation contains abstracts of slave importation affidavits for nine Georgia counties where these affidavits were either recorded in their own volume (i.e. register) or were otherwise kept together in a discrete set, namely: Camden County, Columbia County, Elbert County, Franklin County, Jackson County, Jasper County, Morgan County, Pulaski County, and Wilkes County. Information on the location of each county's records is found under that county's section. Unless otherwise noted in the introductory section, the original register is held in the Clerk of the Superior Court's office in the seat of the county in question, as far as is known.

The registers for a tenth county, Richmond County, will be published in a future volume.

Officials in other counties likely complied with the same laws as those in these ten counties, but recorded affidavits in other court volumes rather than creating a self-contained volume for these affidavits. Alternatively, it is entirely possible that records in other counties were destroyed or lost over time.

Even within the counties named, affidavits may have been recorded in other court records, or found loose, in addition to those found within the discrete sets abstracted herein. No attempt was made by the compiler to search for such separate recordings due to the large volume of extant court records available for the named counties. The diligent researcher would be wise to keep a weather eye open for this possibility.

These affidavits were based on an 1817 law regulating the slave trade in Georgia, which was in turn based on an earlier federal law. In Georgia, the law was repealed and re-enacted several times between 1817 and 1855, when it was repealed for the final time.

METHODOLOGY

Each record generally contains two parts: the affidavit of the person bringing slaves into the state and the certificate showing that the intention to introduce the named slaves into the state has been reported to the appropriate official. Not all records contain these two parts, but many do, and each may contain slightly different information. These two parts were abstracted together, where both were included. Any varying information is noted.

Additionally, another certificate may have been recorded stating that the named slaves had actually been brought into the state. This certificate was most often done in Camden and Columbia Counties, but other counties may have recorded this certification. The second certificate was abstracted herein as a separate record, since it was often recorded well after the original affidavit and certificate.

Information abstracted includes the name of the person bringing slaves into the state, the date of this event, the names of slaves, and any descriptive information about the slaves. The latter usually included the age, gender, complexion, and occupation, although not always. All information was retained in the order in which it was given within each individual record.

Of particular importance are any relationships specified between individual slaves, either stated directly or implied from the order in which the slaves were listed within each affidavit.

Other information included in the original record might be the place of origin, physical descriptions beyond those mentioned above, and specific reasons for bringing slaves into the state (e.g. on behalf of another person). This information was included herein where ever it was mentioned in the original.

Many affidavits appear to bear the original signature of the deponent. Such instances were not noted individually, but every attempt was made here to render as faithful an interpretation of original signatures and marks as possible.

Each county recorded information about incoming slaves in a different order, and this order was retained. The transition in reading these entries from one county to the next might thus be difficult, but the benefits of maintaining the integrity of the original record outweigh the shortcomings inherent in creating a uniform abstraction. In any case, and whenever possible, items were abstracted so that each retained a narrative flow in the hopes of improving readability.

Some punctuation was added or altered as needed. Generally speaking, semi-colons were used to distinguish between information on the various individuals named, particularly in longer affidavits or in affidavits where information was given in columns. In the latter case, ditto marks were often used. To render a more readable copy, the ditto marks were omitted here but replaced with items they, in turn, replaced. Please see the original records.

Referenced page numbers refer always to pages in the original volume. Names were placed in bold type herein (although they were not "bolded" in the originals) in order to highlight them so that they may be found more easily. The spelling of names was left exactly as it was found in the original, or as close as possible, with questionable interpretations noted.

EXAMPLE

What follows is a full transcription of one affidavit to serve as an example of the differences between the original affidavits and the abstracts contained herein.

> Georgia, Elbert County. Clerks office Sup[r] Court. George Evenson being duly Sworn saith that he is about to bring and introduce into this State the following negro Slaves in terms of an act of the Legislature of this State passed on the twentieth of Dec[r] 1817 & revised in 1829 to restrict and regulate the introduction of Slaves into this State for sale &c. to Wit Silvy a female about twenty two years old & Jincy a female Child about four months old both dark Complected, That he is the true and

lawful owner of said Slaves, that said Slaves are about to be brought and introduced into this State for the sole purpose of being held to service and labour by him his heirs Executors administrators or legatees &c. & Without any intent to Sell, transfer barter lend hire Mortgage procure to be taken & Sold under Execution or other legal process so as to vest the use or Service or labour in any other person or persons for the life time of said Slaves, or for any other period of time or in any Way or Manner to defeat avoid or elude the true intent and meaning of said act. Sworn to and Subscribed before me this 18th Nov 1831

    Richard L Aycock J. P. } George Eavenson

[Source: Elbert County, Georgia, Affidavits for bringing slaves into the state, Book A, 1822 – 1847: 55; Clerk of the Superior Court, Elberton; Georgia Archives microfilm drawer 2, box 76.]

See also the three images of affidavits referenced in "List of Illustrations."

ACKNOWLEDGMENTS

Many thanks to the following individuals for their help in compiling this volume.

My son, Caleb, for his patience.

My father, Varney, and brother, David, who each agreed to allow Caleb to look after them so I could work.

Richard E. Hopkins, Jr., for being a sounding board at all hours of the day and night.

Linda Woodward Geiger and Michael Hait, who each offered advice on abstracting, formatting, and otherwise handling these records.

David E. Paterson, who was in part, and unknowingly, an inspiration for the pursuit of a published abstract of these records.

The staff, past and present, of the Georgia Archives in Morrow for their help in locating original affidavits and registers held by the Archives.

CAMDEN COUNTY
1818 – 1847

Slave importation affidavits for this county were recorded in "Camden County Affidavits Made by Owners Bringing Slaves into the State, 1818 – 1847." This volume appears to contain the original signatures of the deponents. It is located on microfilm in two places at the Georgia Archives: on the reel located at drawer 71, box 23; and on the reel located at drawer 27, box 14. The boxes' exterior labels make it appear as if these films contain two separate records, but they are, in fact, copies of the same volume. If using the microfilm to obtain full copies of these records, film 27/14 is by far superior to film 71/23.

The scribe often used tables to describe the attributes of each slave, and "Ditto," "Do," or quotation marks to represent information already stated. Because the tabular format was not retained during the abstraction process, and to avoid confusion, the quoted information is given here instead of the ditto marks.

In this county, the slave holders often made two reports to the court: the first being the affidavit and certificate, and the second being a report that the slaves had actually been brought into the state. While the affidavit and certificate were abstracted as one document (because they were part and parcel of the process), the second reporting to the court was abstracted separately, when given.

Pages 54, 59, 76, 81, 144, 146, 148, 150, and 152 were left blank in the original volume.

Pages 1 – 2: Georgia, Camden County. **John Belleme** of South Carolina being Sworn saith that it is his intention to Settle and Resid in Camden County, Georgia and that it is his intention to bring into the State Twenty One negro Slaves from South Carolina: **Nero** male 25 years old, 5 feet 6 inches, Black Complexion[?]; **Tom** male 21, 5 feet 8 inches, yellow; **Jack** male 21, 5 feet 6 inches, Black; **Ben** male 18, 5 feet 0 inches, Black; **Nero** male 17, 5 feet 2 inches, Black; **Sipio** male 13, 5 feet 0 inches, Black; **Peter** male 13, 5 feet 0 inches, Black; **Friday** male 8, 4 feet 6 inches, Black; **Nancy** female 20, 5 feet 6 inches, Black; **Lidia** female 18, 5 feet 1 inches, Black; **Phillis** female 5 feet 2 inches, Black; **Crisia** female 14, 5 feet 0 inches, Black; **Bella** female 50, 6 feet 0 inches, Black; **Maria** female 10, 4 feet 4 inches, Black; **Celia** female 3, 2 feet 0 inches, Black; **Cudger** male 19, 6 feet 0 inches, yellow; **Ellich** male 17, 5 feet 0 inches, Black; **Anthony** male 10, 4 feet 2 inches, Black; **Tancy** male 8, 4 feet 2 inches, Black; **Joe** male 7, 4 feet 0 inches, yellow; **Stephen** male 14, 5 feet 0 inches, Black. 14 March 1818. /s/ John Belleme.

Pages 3 – 4: Georgia, Camden County. **G. A. Cox** of South Carolina being Sworn Saith that it is his intention to Settle and Reside in Camden, County Georgia aforesaid and that it is his intention to bring into the State four Negro Slaves from South Carolina: **Bob** male 27 years old, 5 feet 6 ½ inches, Black; **Jacob** male 20, 5 feet 10 inches, Black; **Clara** female 16, 5 feet 5 inches, Black; **Hester**[?] female 12, 5 feet 1 ½ inches, Black. 12 January 1819. /s/ G A Cox.

Pages 4 – 5: Georgia, Camden County. **Thomas Hall** of South Carolina but at present of Camden County being Sworn Saith that it is his intention to Settle and Reside in Camden County and that it is his intention to bring into Georgia Sixteen Negro Slaves from South Carolina: **John** Thirty Six years of age Black Complec^d.; **Baccas** Twenty Three Black; **Mary** Thirty Black; **Sarah** Twenty Three Black; **Charlot** Twenty Three, Pegnant [*sic*], Black; **Rose** Fifteen Pregnant Black; **Fib** Eleven Black; **Hannah** nine Black; **Jinny** Six Black; **Silvy** Four Black; **Andos**[?] Three Black; **Winny** nine years of age yellow Complection; **Tiner** Seven years Black; **Hager** Five Black; **Joe** Two Black; **Ben** Thirteen Black. 17 April 1820. /s/ Thomas Hall.

Pages 6 – 7: Georgia, Camden County. **D. L. Clinch** late of North Carolina being sworn saith that it is his intention to Reside in the county and State aforesaid and that it is his intention to bring into the State five Negro slaves from Virginia: **Daniel** yellow complection 28 years of age; **Walace** yellow 19; **Alfred** yellow 7; **Delphi** Black 33; **Sarah** Black 14. 29 January 1821. /s/ D. L. Clinch.

Page 7: Georgia, Camden County. **Archibald Clark** of Camden County being Sworn Saith that he is about to introduce into the State Two negro men Slaves aged about forty to forty five years Each named **Ben** and **Joe** (by trade [smudged] Caulkers). 30 July 1821. /s/ Arch^d Clark.

Pages 8 – 9: Georgia. **Reme Brunett** a Free man of Color of Camden County being Sworn Saith that he is about to introduce into the State from the Province of East Floridia now a Part of the United States Two negro Slaves: **Lydia** about Twenty one years of age and her Child named **Prince** about three months of age. 2 August 1821. /s/ R. Brunett. **Archibald Clark** Esquire Guardian of Reme Brunett a Free man of Color of The Town of St. Marys Saith That the facts Set forth in the foregoing affidavit he beleevs to be true. 11 October 1821. /s/ Arch^d Clark.

Pages 10 – 11: Georgia. **Joshua Hickman** of Camden County being Sworn Saith that he is about to introduce into the State from the Province of East Floridia now a part of the United States Eighteen negro Slaves: **Jim** aged about Twenty five years; **Harry** Thirteen years; **Sam** Seventeen years; **Ben** Seventeen years; **Jeffrey** Ten years; **Jacob** fourteen years; **Jack** Ten years; **Isaac** Sixteen years; **Robert** Thirteen years; **Paul** Sixteen years; **Glass** Eleven years; **Sharp** fifteen years; **Indy** Thirty years; **Jinney** thirteen years; **Hannah** fourteen; **Clarisa** fourteen years; **Fanney** Thirteen years; and **Peggy** Thirteen years; being Eighteen in number and (field hands or laborers). 2 August 1821. [No signature.]

Pages 12 – 13: Georgia. **William Colson** of Camden County being Sworn Saith that he has brought into the State from the Province of East Floridia now a Part of the United States of America a Negro Man named **Romea** about Twenty four years of age and of a Black Complection. 6 August 1821. /s/ Wm Colson.

Pages 13 – 14: Georgia, Camden. **Robert Ripley** of Camden County being Sworn Saith that he is about to introduce into the State from the Province of East Floridia now a part of the United States one negro Slave named **Mely** about Twelve years of age. 2 August 1821. /s/ Robert Ripley.

Pages 14 – 15: Georgia. **John Bachlott** of Camden County being Sworn Saith that he is about to introduce into the State from the Province of East Floridia now a part of the United States a Negro boy named **Coco** fifteen years of age. 2 August 1821. /s/ John Bachelot[?].

Pages 15 – 17: Georgia, Camden County. **William Gibson** [later Esquire] of the Town of St. Marys State having been Sworn deposeth that he is about to bring into this State the following Slaves belonging to him: **Mary Ann** a woman about 35 years of age; and her children, **Pheby** about Ten years; **Cupid** about Eight; **Flora** about Six; and **Affy**[?] about Three; **Ben** about Eleven years of age; **Eliza** about Ten years. Slaves received as a part of the property of his late Wife. 11 August 1821. /s/ Willm. Gibson. [Slaves] from the Province of East Floridia now a Part of the United States of America and to be located in Camden County.

Pages 17 – 18: Georgia, Camden County. **Israel Barber** of Camden County being Sworn Saith that he is about to introduce into this State Two negro men Slaves named **Richard** and **Tom** the former aged about Twenty two years by trade a Laborer the other aged about Thirty years by trade a Ship Carpenter. From the Province of East Floridia now a part of the United States. 14 August 1821. /s/ Israel Barber.

Pages 18 – 19: Georgia, Camden County. **Louis Dufour** of the Town of St. Marys Merchant being Sworn Saith That he is the lawful owner of a Certain slave named **Alexander** now in the Province of East Floridia part of the United States that he is about to introduce Alexander aged about Nineteen years Five feet five Inch high. 8 September 1821. /s/ Louis Dufour.

Pages 19 – 20: Georgia, Camden County. **Mary J. P. Atkinson** of Camden County being Sworn Saith that She is about to introduce into this State two Slaves: **George** aged about nineteen (black Complexion) a field hand; and **Philip** aged about Forty years (black Complexion) a field hand. 22 September 1821. /s/ Mary J P Atkinson. [Brought] from the

Province of East Floridia now a part of the United States of America and to be located in Camden County.

Page 21: Georgia, Camden County. **Archibald Clark** being Sworn Deposeth That the negro Slaves **Ben & Joe** as reported to the Clerk of the Superior Court of the County aforesaid on the Thirtieth day of July last past have been introduced Within the Said County. 11 October 1821. /s/ Arch^d. Clark. The Two negro men Slaves by Trade (Caulkers).

Pages 22: Georgia, Camden County. **John Bashlott** of the Town of Saint Marys being Sworn deposeth That the negro Slave named **Coco** as reported to the Clerk of the Superior Court of the County aforesaid on the Second day of August last past has been introduced Within the Said County. 11 October 1821. /s/ John Bachelott[?].

Pages 23: Georgia, Camden County. **Louis Dufour** of the town of Saint Marys being sworn sayeth that the negro Slave named **Alexander** as Reported to the clerk of the Superior Court of the county aforesaid on the Eighth day of September last past have been introduced within the said county. 11 October 182[1]. /s/ Louis Dufour.

Pages 24 – 25: Georgia, Camden County. **Isarall Barber** Esquire of Said County being Sworn Saith that he is the lawful owner of a negro Slave named **Roger** now in the province of East Floridia part of the United States of America That he is about to introduce Roger aged about Twelve years. 1 December 1821. /s/ Israel Barber.

Pages 25 – 28: State of Georgia, Camden County. **William Berrie** [later Esquire] being Sworn Saith that he is the Lawful owner of negro Slaves named: **Lucy** about Thirty years of age; **Peggy** about Eleven years of age; **Lucy** about nine years of age; **Billy** about Two years of age; **Amy** about Seven years of age; **Dianah** about Thirty years of age; **Smart** about Ten years of age; **Amy** about nine years of age; and **Christmas** about Two years of age. Nine in number now in the Province of East Floridia now a part of the United States of America. 6 December 1821. /s/ Willm Berrie.

Pages 28 – 29: Georgia, Camden County. **William Gibson** Esquire of Said County bing Sworn Sayeth That the negro Slaves named **Maryann, Phebe, Cupid, Flora**, and **Affey** being a Part of the negro Slaves as Reported to the Clerk of the Superior Court of Camden County on the Eleventh day of August last past have been introduced within the Said county. 9 January 1822. /s/ Willm. Gibson.

Pages 29 – 30: Georgia, Camden County. **Mary J. P. Atkinson** of Camden County being Sworn Sayeth that the negro Slaves **George** and **Phillip** the Two negro Slaves reported to the Clerk of the Superior Court of Camden County on the Twenty Second day of September Eighteen hundred and Twenty one have been introduced within the Said County. 23 February 1822. /s/ Mary J P Atkinson.

Page 30: Georgia, Camden County. **Israel Barber** being Sworn Sayeth that the following named negro Slaves **Tom**[,] **Dick & Roger** as reported to the Clerk of the Superior Court of Camden County the Said Tom & Dick reported on the 14th August last past and Roger reported on the 1st day of December last past have been brought into this State and County. 20 March 1822. /s/ Israel Barber.

Pages 31 – 32: Georgia, Camden County. **William Gibson** [later Esquire] being sworn Sayeth that he is the lawful owner of a certain negro Slave named **Patty** [later Pattey] & her children **Amy**, **Louisa**, **Dick** and **Dublin** which he [illegible] to introduce into this State. 20 March 1822. /s/ Will[m] Gibson. [Brought] from the Province of East Floridia now a Part of the United States.

Pages 33 – 34: State of Georgia, Camden County. **Noel Raulerson** of Appling County being Sworn Saith that he is the lawful owner of a negro man Slave named **Abraham** now about to be brought from the province of East Floridia a part of the United States of America, aged about Thirty years. 18 March 1822. /s/ Noel Raulerson.

Page 34: Georgia, Camden County. Copy of Certificate Granted to **Israel Barber**. Israel Barber Esquire, having declared oath before me, hath by virtue of Two Certificates Granted him one on the 14th day of August last past and the other on the 1st day of December last past Introduced and brought in the following negro Slaves **Tom**[,] **Dick & Roger** reported as aforesaid. 30 March 1822.

Pages 35 – 37: Georgia, Camden County. **Louis** [later Lewis] **Dufour** of the Town of St. Marys being Sworn doth Say that he is the lawful owner of the following negroe Slaves now in the Province of East Floridia: **Cumbo** and her child **Pussey** and **Helen** aged about Twenty three years; Cumbo about thirty and her child Pussey about Seven years. 15 March 1822. /s/ Louis Dufour.

Pages 38 – 41: Georgia, Camden County. **Joseph Woodruff** [later Major Joseph Woodruff] of Said State being Sworn Doth Say that he is the lawful owner of the following negro Slaves about to be imported and introduced into this State from Virginia: **Harry** 5' 3 ¾", 40 years Black; **James** 5' 5 ½", 40 years yellow; **Bobb** 5' 7 ¾", 38 yellow; **Billy** 5 8 ½", 42 Black; **Bill** 5' 9 ¾", 22 Black; **Charles** 5' 2", 28 Black; **Phebe** 5' 2", 22 Black; **Infant** 3' 1 ¼", 4 yellow; **Ceesar** 5' 2 ½", 22 Black; **Fanny** 5' 3", 20 Black; **Infant** 6 months Black; **Lewis** 5' 4 ½", 55 years Black; **Nancy** 4' 11 ¾", 56 years Black; **Betsey** 4' 5", 13 yellow; **Hannah** 4' 2 ¾", 10 Black; **Lucy** 4' ½", 8 Black; **Tom** 4' 7 ¾", 12 Black; **Joe** 4' -", 8 yellow; **Letty** 5' 1 ¼", 40 Black; **Lucy** 5' ¾", 26 Black; **Sam** 4' 1 ¼", 9 Black; **Dinah** 3' 9 ½", 7 Black; **George** 2' 8", 3 Mulatto; **Julia** 5' 1", 23 Black; **Henry** 2' 10", 1 ½ Black; **Jacob** 5' 4", 32 yellow; **Harriot** 5' 3", 25 Mulatto; **Mary** 3' 1 ½", 3 Mulatto; **Jonathan** 2' 7", 1 ¾ Mulatto; **Sally** 5' 1 ¼", 25 Black; **Mary** 3' 8", 5 Black; **William** 3' 1 ¾", 3 yellow; **Abraham** 2' 6 ¼", 2 yellow. 4 March 1822. /s/ J. Woodruff.

Pages 41 – 42: Georgia, Camden County. **Joseph Desclaux** of the Town of St. Marys being Sworn doth Say that he is the lawful owner of the following negro Slaves now in the Province of East Floridia: **John** a boy about Thirteen years of age; and **Caty** a Girl about Thirteen years of age. 10 May 1822. /s/ Joseph Descloux, his mark "+".

Pages 43 – 44: Georgia, Camden County. **George W. Martin** of the Town of St. Marys being Sworn doth Say that he is the lawful owner of the negro man about Twenty years of age Named **Aleck** now in the province of East Floridia that the deponant is about to bring and introduce Said Slave into Camden County in the State aforesaid. 11 May 1822. /s/ Geo. W. Martin.

Pages 44 – 45: Georgia, Camden County. **William Bailey** of the County and State aforesaid being Sworn doth Say that he is the lawful owner of the following Slaves now in the Province of East Floridia: **Russell** and **Jacob** the former about forty five or fifty years of age and the latter about Twenty or Twenty five years of age Russell a mulatto and Jacob a Black Complection that the deponant is about to bring and introduce Said Slaves into Camden County in the State aforesaid. 21 May 1822. /s/ Wᵐ Bailey.

Pages 45 – 46: Georgia, Camden County. **William Gibson** Esquire of the Town of St. Marys being Sworn doth Say that he is the Lawful owner of a negro Slave named **Joe** now in the Province of East Floridia that the deponant is about to bring and introduce Said Slave into Camden County in the State aforesaid. 4 June 1822. /s/ Willᵐ. Gibson.

Page 47: Georgia, Camden County. **William Bailey** of the County and State aforesaid being Sworn Sayeth that the Two negro Slaves Slaves **Russell** and **Jacob** as reported to the Clerk of the Superior Court of Camden County on the Twenty first day of May Last past have been introduced into this State. 4 June 1822. /s/ Wᵐ Bailey.

Pages 48 – 49: Georgia, Camden County. **George W. Martin** of St. Marys in the County aforesaid being Sworn Saith that he is at this time possessed of a Negro Slave called **Molly** about the age of thirteen years "of the class of entire Black brought up in the business of a House Servant." 8 June 1822. /s/ Geo. W. Martin.

Pages 49 – 50: Georgia, Camden County. **George W. Marton** being Sworn Sayeth that the negro man named **Aleck** reported to the Clerk of the Superior Court on the Eleventh of May last past and the negro Girl named **Molly** reported to the Said Clerk on the Eighth day of June last past have been under virtue of the Two Certificates Granted by Said Clerk introduced into the State. 10 July 1822. /s/ [Illegible].

Pages 50 – 51: Georgia, Camden County. **Joseph Descloux** of the Town of St. Marys being Sworn Sayeth that the Two negro Slaves named **John** and **Caty** reported to the Clerk of the Superior Court of Said County on the Tenth day of May Last past have been under virtue of the Certificate Granted by the Said Clerk Introduced into the State. 10 July 1822. /s/ Joseph Descloux, his mark "+".

Pages 51 – 53: Georgia, Camden County. **John Chevalier** Having been Sworn deposeth That he is about to introduce into this State a Slave named **Joe** about nineteen years of Age. 21 June 1822. /s/ John Chevalier.

Pages 55 – 57: Georgia, Camden County. **William Berrie** having been Sworn sayeth that he is about to introduce into this State Two negro Slaves **Bob** and **Rose** his Wife Bob about Thirty years of age and Rose about Twenty Eight years of age. 11 November 1822. /s/ Willm Berrie. [Brought] from the province of East Floridia now a part of the United States.

Pages 57 – 58: Georgia, Camden County. **Mary Boisseau** having been Sworn Sayeth That She intends bringing into this State from East Floridia the following negroes: **Daulphin**, **Clarissee**, **Flora**, **Rassee**, **Polaus** and **Juliet** Six in number. 11 October 1822. /s/ Mary Boisseau, her mark [blank].

Pages 60 – 61: Georgia, Camden County. **John C. Richard** being Sworn Sayeth that he intends bringing into this State from East Floridia the following negroes: **Tranquelino**[,] **Clauda** and **August** Three in number. 7 January 1823. /s/ Jno. C. Richard.

Pages 62 – 63: Georgia, Camden County. **Robert Miller** of the County aforesaid being Sworn Saith that he is lawfully possessed of the following negro Slaves: **George** aged about nineteen years; **Jenny** twenty five years; and her child **Marra** [later Mariah] aged 2; **Fanny** aged fourteen years; **Bob** fourteen; **Peter** fifteen; **Quashy** twenty Eight years; **Jim** twenty three years; (all of whom are field hands) that he is about to bring the Same into the State to be located in the County aforesaid from the Territory of East Floridia. 5 February 1823. /s/ Robert Miller.

Pages 64 – 65: Georgia, Camden County. **Robert Miller** being Sworn Saith that the negro Slaves **George**, **Jenney**, **Mariah**, **Fanney**, **Bob**, **Peter**, **Quashey** & **Jim** Eight in number as reported to the Clerk of the Superior Court on the fifth day of February last past have been under virtue of the Certificate Granted by the Said Clerk Introduced into this State from the Territory of East Floridia for to be Located in the County aforesaid. 17 July 1823. /s/ Robert Miller.

Page 65 – 66: Georgia, Camden County. **William Gibson** of the County aforesaid being Sworn Saith that he is the lawfull owner of a negro Slave named **Smart** aged about Thirty Three years that he is about to introduce the Said negro into this State to be located in the County aforesaid from the Territory of East Floridia. 21 February 1823. /s/ Willm. Gibson.

Page 67: Georgia, Camden County. **William Gibson** Esquire being Sworn Sayeth that the negro man Slave named **Smart** as reported to the Clerk of the Superior Court on the Twenty first day of February last past have been under and by virtue of the Certificate Granted by the Said Clerk Introduce and brought into the this State and County aforesaid from the Territory of East Floridia. 3 March 1823. /s/ Willm. Gibson.

Pages 68 – 69: Georgia, Camden County. **William Gibson** having been Sworn Saith that he is about to introduce into the State a negro man Slave named **Scipio** about Twenty four years of Age a field hand. 28 March 1823. /s/ Willm. Gibson. [To be brought] from the Territory of East Floridia.

Page 69: Georgia, Camden County. **William Gibson** Esquire being Sworn Sayeth that the negro man Slave named **Scipio** as reported to the Clerk of the Superior Court on the Twenty Eigth [sic] day of March last past has been under virtue of the Certificate Granted by the said Clerk Introduced and brought into this State from the Territory of East Floridia. 6 May 1823. /s/ Willm. Gibson.

Pages 70 – 71: Georgia, Camden County. **James King** of Said County having been Sworn Sayeth that he is about to introduce into the State a negro Woman Slave named **Terrasa** and her child **Hannah**, the Said negro woman about Eighteen years of age and her child about one year old. 5 April 1823. /s/ James King. [To be brought] from the Territory of East Floridia.

Pages 72 – 73: Georgia, Camden County. **Andrew N. Johnston** of Wayne County having been Sworn Sayeth that he intends bringing into this State from the Territory of East Floridia the following Negro Slaves: **Frank** about Seventeen years of age Black Complection; **Mingo** about Sixteen years of age yellow Complection; **Nancey** a Girl about Thirteen years of age Black Complection; and **Mariah** a Girl about nine or ten years of age Black Complection. 16 May 1823. /s/ Andrew N Johnston.

Pages 74: Copy of Certificate Granted to **William Gibson**. Georgia, Camden County. William Gibson Esquire having declared on Oath before me that he hath under virtue of the Certificate Granted him on the Eighth day of March last past Introduced into this State and County aforesaid the negro man **Sipio**. 6 May 1823.

Pages 74 – 75: Georgia, Camden County. **Reme Brunett** being Sworn Saith that he is about to Introduce into this State from the Territory of East Floridia a negro woman named **Caty** aged about nineteen years yellow Complection a common field Hand. 14 November 1823. /s/ R. Brunett.

Pages 77 – 78: Georgia, Camden County. **William Gibson** Esquire of Said County being Sworn Saith that he is about to introduce into this State from the Territory of East Floridia

Three negro Slaves: **Smart[,] Tom & Eve** all Black Complection. Smart aged about Twenty years; Tom aged about Thirty five years; & Eve about Sixteen years; all common field hands. 15 November 1823. /s/ Willm. Gibson.

Pages 78 – 79: Georgia, Camden County. **William Gibson** being Sworn Saith that the negroes **Smart[,] Tom & Eve** as reported to the Clerk of the Superior Court on the fifteenth day of November last have been under virtue of the Certificate Granted him by the Said Clerk Introduced into this State from the Territory of East Floridia. 5 January 1824. /s/ Willm. Gibson.

Pages 79 – 80: Georgia, Camden County. **William Bailey** of Said County being Sworn Saith that he is about to Introduce into this County and State: **Ben** about Twenty Two years of age; **Lydia** about Twenty years; **Claremon** about nineteen years; **Petty** about thirteen years; **Frank** about Twelve years; **Hampton** about 2 years. 7 January 1824. /s/ Wm Bailey.

Pages 82 – 83: Georgia, Camden County. **Richard Lang** of Said County being Sworn Saith that he is about to introduce into this State and County The following negro Slaves: **Eraw** about Thirty years of age Yellow Complection; **Sarah** about Twenty five or Thirty years of age Yellow Complection; **Clarrisa** about fourteen years of age Dark Complection; from the Territory of Floridia. 4 February 1824. /s/ Richard Lang.

Pages 83 – 84: Georgia, Camden County. **Richard Lang** being Sworn Saith that the negroes **Eraw[,] Sarah & Clarrisy** as reported to the Clerk of the Superior Court on the fourth Instant have been under virtue of the Certificate Granted him by the Said Clerk Introduced into this State and County from the Territory of Floridia. 11 Febuary 1824. /s/ Richard Lang.

Pages 85 – 86: Georgia, Camden County. **William Gibson** Esquire of Said County being Sworn Saith that he is about to Introduce into this County and State from the Territory of Floridia the following negro Slaves: **Peter** about forty five years of age **Tom** and **Dolley** his wife **Nanny[,] William & Sarah** their Children; **Cesar[,] Jinny** & their daughter **Sophia**; **George** about Thirty years of Age. 7 February 1824. /s/ Willm. Gibson.

Pages 86 – 87: Georgia, Camden County. **William Gibson** Esquire being Sworn Saith that the negro Slaves **Peter, Tom, Dolley, Nanny, William, Sarah, Cesar, Jenney, Sophia & George** as reported to the Clerk of the Superior Court on the Seventh Instant have been under virtue of the Certificate Granted him by the Said Clerk Introduced into this State and County from the Territory of Floridia. 19 February 1824. /s/ Willm. Gibson.

Pages 87 – 89: Georgia, Camden County. **William Gibson** Esquire Executor of the Estate of **Ambrose Hull** of Said County being Sworn Saith that he is about to introduce into this County and State from the Territory of Floridia the following negro Slaves: **Patience** about Eighteen years of age mulatto[?] Complection and her child **Polly** about Two years of age and **Ellen** about fifteen years of Age mulatto Complection. 7 February 1824. /s/ Willm. Gibson.

Pages 89 – 90: Georgia, Camden County. **William Gibson** esquire Executor of the Estate **Ambrose Hull** of Said County being Sworn Saith that the negro Slaves **Patience**[,] **Polly** & **Ellen** as reported to the Clerk of the Superior Court on the Seventh Instant have been under virtue of the Certificate Granted him by Said Clerk Introduced into this State and County from the Territory of Floridia. 19 February 1824. /s/ Willm. Gibson.

Pages 90 – 91: Georgia, Camden County. **Samuel Clark** one of the firm of Clarke & Brown being Sworn Saith that they are about to Introduce into this County and State from the Territory of Floridia the following negro Slaves: **Joe** about Thirty five years of age and his daughter **Amelia** about thirteen years of Age. 7 February 1824. /s/ S. Clarke.

Page 92: Georgia, Camden County. **Samuel Clarke** one of the firm of Clarke & Brown being Sworn Saith that the negro Slaves **Joe** and **Amelia** as reported to the Clerk of the Superior Court of Said County on the Seventh Instant have been udner virtue of the Certificate Granted them by Said Clerk Introduced into the State and County from the Territory of Floridia. 20 February 1824. /s/ S. Clarke.

Pages 93 – 94: Georgia, Camden County. **Whipple Aldrich** of Said County being Sworn Saith that he is about to introduce into the State and County from the Territory of Floridia a negro woman named **Caty** about Twenty one years of Age, not exactly Dark Complection. 6 February 1824. /s/ Whipple Aldrich.

Pages 94 – 95: Georgia, Camden County. **Whipple Aldrich** being Sworn Saith that the negro woman **Caty** as reported to the Clerk of the Superior Court on the Sixth Instant has been under virtue of the Certificate Granted him by Said Clerk Introduced into this State and County from the Territory of Floridia. 20 February 1824. /s/ Whipple Aldrich.

Pages 95 – 96: Georgia, Camden County. **Reme Brunett** of Said County being Sworn Saith that he is about to introduce from the Territory of East Floridia a negro man **Jacob** about Twenty four years of age dark Complection. 6 September 1824. [No signature.]

Pages 97 – 98: Georgia, Camden County. **Y. L. Robinson** attorney of **A. D. Jones** Trustee for **Jane B. Robinson** being Sworn Saith that he has Introduced into this State and County from South Carolina the following Negroes: **Billy**[?], **Nelly**, **Marth**, **Reuben**, **Betty**, **Charles**, **John**, **Frank**, **John**, **Will**, **Aleck**, **George**, **Sylvia**, **Mary**, **Sal**, **Jorden**, **Henry**, **Caroline**, **Edward**[?], **Frances**, **Sarah**, **Voilet**, **Sal**, **Ned**, **Dorcas**, **Cato**, **Hiram**. That the Said Negroes are brought into this State for the Sole use of Jane B. Robinson & her heirs. 25 February 1830. /s/ Y. L. Robinson.

Pages 98 – 99: Georgia, Camden County. **Silvester Silva** being Sworn Saith that he has introduced into the State and County aforesaid from the State of South Carolina The following negro Slaves: **Engenca** a woman aged about Twenty one years; **Dick** a boy aged about thirteen years; and **Nancy** a woman about thirty years of age; all of Black Complection. 13 May 1830. /s/ Sillvester[?] Silva.

Pages 99 – 100: Georgia, Camden County. **Joseph Arnow** of said County being Sworn Saith that he is about to introduce into the State and County aforesaid from the Teritory of Florida a negro woman **Harriet** and her child **Rose** both of a dark Complection, the woman about twenty years of age, the child about one months old. 13 May 1830. /s/ Joseph Arnow.

Page 101: Georgia, Camden County. **B. Baratte** being Sworn Saith that he has introduced into the State and County aforesaid from the State of South Carolina a negro Slave named **Sarah** about Seventeen years of age of a dark Complexion. 20 July 1830. /s/ Baratte.

Pages 102 – 103: Georgia, Camden County. **G. W. Thomas** [later George W. Thomas] being Sworn Saith that he intends introducing into this State from Nassaw County East Florida a certain negro Slave named **Harriet** and her child **Rose** both of a Yellow Complexion, the former aged about twenty years & the latter about six months. 15 October 1830. /s/ G W Thomas.

Page 103: Georgia, Camden County. **George W. Thomas** being sworn saith that the negro woman **Harriett** and her child **Rose** as Reported to the Clerk of the Superior Court on the fifteenth day of October last past have been under and by virtue of the certificate Granted by the Clerk introduced and brought into this State and County aforesaid. 6 November 1830. /s/ G W Thomas.

Pages 103 – 104: Georgia, Camden County. **Sylvester Sylvia** being Sworn Saith that he has brought into this State and County aforesaid from the Teritory of Florida a negro boy Slave named **Antonio** about Sixteen or Seventeen years of age, of a black complection. 8 November 1830. /s/ Sillvester Silva.

Page 105: Georgia, Camden County. Mrs. **Catherine Barnardy** being sworn Saith that she is about to introduce into this State and County aforesaid from the teritory of East Florida a negro girl Slave named **Sarah** about Seventeen years of age of a Black Complection. 14 December 1830. /s/ C. Bernardy.

Page 106: Georgia, Camden County. **Henry Bacon** being Sworn Saith that he has introduced into this State and County aforesaid a negro man Slave named **Wilson** from East Florida about twenty five years of age of a Black complextion. 29 December 1830. /s/ H Bacon.

Page 107: Georgia, Camden County. **Richard Lang** being Sworn Saith that he has introduced into this State and County aforesaid a negro man Slave from the teritory of East Florida named **Charles** about thirty years of age of a Yellowish Complextion. 11 February 1831. /s/ Richard Lang.

Page 108: Georgia, Camden County. **D[?]. Baratte** being Sworn Saith he has introduced from the teritory of Florida a negro woman Slave named **Chloe** about twenty Seven years of age of a black complextion also her daughter **Sarah** about Seven years of age of a black Complextion. 29 August 1831. /s/ Baratte. [sic]

Page 109: Georgia, Camden County. **John Bachlott Junior** being sworn Saith that he has introduced to this State and County aforesaid from the Teritory of Florida a negro woman Slave named **Hester** about Eighteen years of age and her boy child **Sam**, about one year old both of a black Complextion. 11 November 1831. /s/ John Bachlott Jun[?].

Page 110: Georgia, Camden County. **James Armstrong** being Sworn Saith that he has introduced into the State and County aforesaid from the teritory of Florida a negro man Slave named **George** about twenty five or thirty years of age of a yellowish Complection. 7 January 1832. /s/ James Armstrong.

Page 111: Georgia, Camden County. **John W. Dubose** being sworn Saith that he has introduced into the State and County aforesaid from the State of South Carolina the following negro Slaves: **Jack**, **Zach**, **Franky**, **Latta**, **Hector**, **Betsey**, **Smart**, **Ann**, **Molly**, **Billy**, **Wiley**, **Martin**, **Jinney**, **Pompys**, **Peggy**, & **Silvia**. 28 January 1832. /s/ John W. DuBose.

Page 112: Georgia, Camden County. **John D. McKindree** being Sworn Saith that he has introduced into the State and County aforesaid from the state of South Carolina the following negro Slaves: **Cretia** and **Charles**. 18 February 1832. /s/ John D McKindree.

Page 113: Georgia, Camden County. **C. M. Caldwell** being Sworn Saith that he has introduced into this State and County aforesaid from the state of South Carolina two negro women[?]: **Tener** and **Mila**. 2 June 1832. /s/ C. M. Caldwell.

Page 114: Georgia, Camden County. **Samuel Clarke** one of the firm of Samuel Clarke & Co being Sworn Saith that they have introduced into this State and County aforesaid from the Teritory of Florida a negro boy named **John** about Seventeen years old. 4 June 1832. s/s S. Clarke.

Page 115: Georgia, Camden County. **John Bailey** being Sworn Saith that he has this day introduced into this State and County aforesaid from the teritory of Florida a negro man named **Jeffery** about Twenty three years of age of a dark complexion. 7 February 1833. /s/ John Bailey.

Page 116: Georgia, Camden County. **Alexander Bachtoll** of the County being Sworn deposeth that he is the lawful owner (in right of his wife) of the following Slaves which he is about to bring into the county aforesaid from the teritory of Florida: **Louisa**, Black, aged 35 years, 5 ft. 6 [inches]; **May**, Black, 12, 4' 6"; **Sam**, Black, 10, 4' 0"; **Amelia**, Black, 4, 3' 0"; **Joe**, Black, 3, 2' 6"; **Moses**, Black, 3, 2' 6". 9 March 1833. /s/ Alexander Bachtoll.

Page 117: Georgia, Camden County. **William McKindree** of the County aforesaid being Sworn Saith that he is the lawful owner of the following Slaves which he has introduced into the County aforesaid from the State of South Carolina: **Sally & Wharley** both of dark complextion. 29 April 1833. /s/ William McKindree.

Page 118: Georgia, Camden County. **William McKindree[?]** of the County aforesaid being Sworn Saith that he is the lawful owner of the following negro Slaves which he has introduced into this State from the State of South Carolina: **Peter** aged about forty five years; **Bella** aged about thirty five years; and **John** aged about nine years; all of Dark Complection. 3 August 1833. /s/ Wm McKendree.

Page 119: Georgia, Camden County. **John Bailey** of the county aforesaid being Sworn Saith that he is the lawful owner of a Negro boy Slave named **Frank** about Sixteen years of age and of a dark Complextion (from the Teritory of East Florida). 29 November 1833. /s/ John Bailey.

Page 120: Georgia, Camden County. **William T. Hopkins** of the county aforesaid being Sworn Saith that he is the lawful owner of the following Negro Slaves: **Ishmael** about fifty five years of age; **Lavenia** about fifty five years of age; **Prince** about twenty three years of age; **Colerain** about forty years of age; **Levenia** about Twenty and an infant **child** [not named] about five years of age; **Lucy** about Seventeen years of age; **Juba** about Eighteen years of age; all of dark or black complextion which he has introduced into this State from the Teritory of East Florida. 10 February 1834. /s/ William T. Hopkins.

Page 121: Georgia, Camden County. **John Pottle** of the county aforesaid being Sworn Saith that he is the lawful owner of a negro boy Slave named **Peter** of a black Complection about fifteen years, which he has introduced into this State from the teritory of Florida. 14 February 1834. /s/ John Pottle.

Page 122: Georgia, Camden County. **William McKindree** of the county aforesaid being Sworn Saith that he is the lawful owner of the following negro Slaves: **Nanny** a woman about twenty two years of age of a black complexion and **Cretia** about twenty one years of age of a Yellow Complexion which he has brought from the State of South Carolina. 1 March 1834. /s/ Wm McKendree.

Page 123: Georgia, Camden County. **Richard Lang** of the county aforesaid being Sworn Saith that he is the lawful owner of the following negro Slaves: **Bob** a man about twenty five years, **Rose** a female his wife aged about thirty two and her two children **Hannah** aged about fifteen years and **Archibald** aged about ten years, the above female aged about fifteen years is a Mulatto the other three are of Black Completion, which negro Slaves have been brought from the territory of Florida. 21 March 1834. /s/ Richard Lang.

Page 124: Georgia, Camden County. **Alexander Bachlott** being duly Sworn Saith that he is the lawful owner of the following negro Slaves: **Ceasar** aged about Sixty years; **Jack** aged about fifty five years; & **Tom** aged about forty five years; all of Black Complexion, which he has brought into this State from the Teritory of Florida. 7 April 1834. /s/ Alexander Bachlott.

Page 125: Georgia, Camden County. **Henry Bacon** being Sworn Saith that he is the lawful owner of the following negro Slaves (ten in number): **Jacob** aged about fifty five years; **Phebe** aged about fifty three years; **Clarinda** aged about twenty five years; **Sarah** aged about Seven years; **Yamma** aged about five years; **Susan** aged about three years; **Daphne** aged about twenty one years; **William** aged about Seven years; **Lewis** aged about three years; **Salina** aged about five months; all of Black complexion Except William of Yellow Complexion, which negro slaves he has brought into this State from the territory of Florida. 7 April 1834. /s/ H Bacon.

Page 126: Georgia, Camden County. **George W. Thomas** being duly Sworn Saith that he is the lawful owner of the following negro Slaves: **Sharper** a man about forty years of age, **Rose** his wife about thirty five years of age and her six children: **Jim**, **Harriet**, **Aaron**, **Jerry**, **Randal**, **Stephen**; all of which negroes are of black complextion, which have been brought into this State from the teritory of Florida. 13 September 1834. /s/ G W Thomas.

Pages 126 – 127: Georgia, Camden Co. **John Bachlott** [later Jno. Backlott] being Sworn Saith that he has introduced into the County and State aforesaid from the Teritory of Florida the following Slaves: **Bog** Black 25 yrs of age; **Jacob** Black 46 age; **Moria** Black 50; **Cornelia** Child yellow 5 yrs of age. 24 January 1835. /s/ John Bachlott.

Page 128: Georgia, Camden County. **Samuel Clarke** being Sworn Saith that he has introduced into this State from the Teritory of East Florida a negro woman named **Betty** aged about forty five years and **Clarissa** aged about nineteen years. 31 January 1835. /s/ S. Clarke.

Page 129: Georgia, Camden County. **Louis Dufore** being Sworn Saith that he has introduced into the State from the Teritory of East Florida: a negro man named **King** aged about Forty years; **Dolly** about thirty five years; **Sam** about 12 years; & **Manuel** aged about twenty; all of black complexion. 31 January 1835. /s/ Louis Dufour.

Page 130: Georgia, Camden County. **Silvester Silva** Guardian for **Harry King** a free man of Colour being Sworn Saith that he has introduced into this State and County from the Teritory of East Florida a negro boy named **Sam** about Eighteen years of age and of Yellow Complextion. 31 January 1835. /s/ Silbestre[?] Silva.

Page 131: Georgia, Camden County. **John M. Geiger** being Sworn Saith that he has introduced into this State from the Teritory of Florida a negro woman named **Suckey** about twenty two years of age and her girl child **Nan** aged about two and a half years both of Black complextion. 9 June 1835. /s/ John M Geiger.

Page 132: **James M. Smith**'s Report of negro Slaves to be introduced into the State of Georgia: **Pompy** a black fellow about 40 old; & **Louisa** his wife Short, black about 40 or 45; **Billy** tall yellow complexion about 30 years old; **Phillis** his wife darck complexion about 38 years old; **Grace** her daughter short brown complexion 18 years old; & **Jim** her son 20 months; **Adam** yellow complexion [illegible] 23 years old; & **Edy** his wife dark complexion 22 years old; & **April** short dark complexion "knockneed" 25 years; & **Lucy** his wife short dark complexion 20 years old; & **Ruckorlas**, tall, dark complexion speaks broken English 50 to 55; & **Rose** his wife yellow complexion 50 to 55 years old; **Harry** short dark square make 45 to 47 years old; **Mary** his wife brown complexion 45 years old; & **Patty** her daughter brown square made 26 years old; **Cuffy** dark complexion 24 years old; **Lizzy** black 20 years old; **Click** [or **Elick**] black square made 17 years old; **Jimy** dark complexion stout 20 years old; **Peggy** light complexion stout 20 years old; **Adam**, carpenter, yellow complexion square make 35 years old; **Jingo**, tall, yellow 25 years old; & **Bina** his wife middling dark 23 years old; **Elvira** small dark complexion about 38 years old; & **Smart** her son, short dark one eye 21 years old; **Jennett** dark complexion scar on her cheek 17 years old; & **Nanny** her sister dark complexion 14 years old; **Kate** tall slender yellow complexion 25 years old; **Tommy** her husband yellow complexion stutters 26 years old; **Josey** short light complexion about 38 or 40 years old; **Hager** dark well made about 38 years old; **Jane** her daughter about 4 old; **Juckolad[?]** a boy 9 years old.

Page 133: State of Georgia, County of Camden. **James Mangen Smith** now of South Carolina being duly sworn saith That he is about to introduce into the state the several Negro slaves annexed and described in the foregoing list with a view to settle and cultivate a Plantation on the Great Satiller River opposite to the Town of Jefferson in the county aforesaid. 30 December 1835. /s/ Jas. M. Smith.

Page 134: Georgia, Camden County. **Silvanus Church** being Sworn Saith that he is about to introduce into this State from the Teritory of Florida a negro woman named **Peggy** & her three children named **Sarah** about Eight years old, **Lucy** aged about four years old & **William** aged about two years, all of Black complextion. 12 January 1837. /s/ Silvanus Church.

Page 135: Georgia, Camden County. **Joseph C. Newberry** being Sworn Saith that he is about to introduce into this State from the teritory of Florida a negro man named **Sandy** about 25 years of age of Dark complextion. 1 November 1837. /s/ Joseph C Newbey[?].

Page 136: Georgia, Camden County. **Samuel J. McKindre** being Sworn saith that he has introduced into this State from Charleston South Carolina: a fellow **Titus** aged 27 years; a woman **Philis** aged forty years; **Eve** aged twenty three years; **Mary** aged 21 years; **Rinah** aged thirty five years; all black. 3 October 1840. /s/ Samuel J McKindree.

Page 137: Georgia, Camden County. **Mrs. Burwell Atkinson** being Sworn Saith that she is about to introduce from the Territory of Florida: **Dick** a man about Sixty five years of age; **Rachiel** a woman about forty five; **Isaac** a boy about twenty two; **Maria** a girl of sixteen; **Jane** a girl of fourteen; **Tom** a boy of twelve; **Rhoda** a girl ten; **Ephraim** a boy of eight; **Alex** a boy of six; **Oseola** a boy of four; **Caroline** a child of two; all black. 19 October 1840. /s/ Ann Atkinson.

Page 138: Georgia, Camden County. **G. W. Thomas** being sworn saith that he intends introducing into this State from Charleston South Carolina a negroe slave named **Rachel**, complexion dark, aged about 11 years. 16 March 1840. /s/ G. W. Thomas.

Page 139: Georgia, Camden County. **George W. Thomas** being sworn saith that he is the lawful owner of the following negroe slave: **Rachel**, complexion dark, aged about eleven years, which negroe slave has been brought into this State from Charleston South Carolina. 15 April 1841. /s/ G. W. Thomas.

Page 140: **Charles J. Cole**'s Report of Slaves ~~to be~~ introduced into the State of Georgia. **David** a light Complection fellow about 30 years; **Amy** his wife Black negroe about 25; **Cinder** about 8 years old their child; **Little David** about 5 years old their child; **Phebee** black woman, about 40[?] years old; **Ishmael** dark complected about 25; **Jimmy** dark complected about 22 years old; **Clifford** dark complected about 30 years old; **Annet[?]** dark complected woman about 24 years old; **Louisa** dark complected woman about 35 years old; **Jacob** dark complected boy about 16 years old; **Ned** dark complected boy about 12 years old; **Adam** dark complected man about 55 years old; **Sharlott** mulatto woman about 50 years old; **Smart** dark complected fellow about 60 years old; **Affy** dark complected woman about 20; **Andrew** dark complected man 24 years old; **Linda** woman dark Complected about 22 years old; **Polly** woman dark complected about 20 years old; **Ben** fellow dark complected about 45 years old; **Clara** mulatto woman about 35 years old; **Isabella** [or Arabella] mulatto woman about 23 years old; **Lucinda** woman mulatto about 20 years old; **Casar[?]** boy 16 years old; **Lemus** boy about 10 years old; **Peter** light complected man 45 years old; **Nelly** dark woman about 31 years old; **Joe** dark complected man 21 years old; **little Peter** boy dark complected 5 years old; **Glascow** boy about 4 years old; **Dick** dark complected man 30 years old; **Tipa[?]** woman dark complected about 28 years old; **Cudjoe** fellow dark complected about 18 years old; **Hector** boy dark 14 years old; **Isaac** boy dark about 10 years old; **Mary Ann** dark 25 years old; **Hager** girl about 8 years old; **Aron** black about 5 years; **Betty** woman about 20 years; **Reuben** light complected fellow about 27 years old; **Hannah** a Mulatto about 23 years old; **Andrew** boy about 4 years old; **little Ben** dark Complected fellow about 16 years old; **June** child dark Complected about 4 years old.

Page 141: Georgia, Camden County. **Charles J. Cole** formerly of South Carolina being sworn saith that he has introduced into the State the several negroe slaves declared in the foregoing list with a [illegible] to settle and cultivate a plantation Brookfield in the County aforesaid. [No date or signature.]

Page 142: Georgia, Camden County. **William Cole** being sworn saith that he is about to introduce into the State from the state of South Carolina: a negroe woman named **Rachael** dark complected woman aged about 25 years old, **Edy** a Girl aged[?] about 6 years old, **Ann** a girl aged about 5, her children. 14 March 1842. /s/ William D Cole.

Page 143: Georgia, Camden County. **J. E. Mizell** being sworn saith that he is the lawful owner of the following negroe Slave: **Eliza** dark complection aged about 16 Years which negroe slave has been brought into this State from Charleston So. Carolina. 12 March 1842. /s/ J. E. Mizell.

Page 143: Georgia, Camden County. **William D. Cole** being sworn saith that he is the lawful owner of the following slaves: **Matilda** 26 years of age dark complection; **Sally** 13 years old dark complection; **Austin** 10 years old; **Sarah** 16 years old; which negroes have been brought into this State from Charleston So. Carolina. 14 March 1842. /s/ William D Cole.

Page 145: Georgia, Camden County. **David John Smith** being sworn saith that he is the lawful owner of the following negro Slaves: **Joe** aged about 38 years; **Toney** aged about 42 years; **Doctor** aged about 20 years; **Jack** aged about 15 years; **Peter** aged about 12 Years; **Hercules** aged about 10 years; **Clarinda** aged about 34 years; **Lucy** aged about 12 years; **Hannah** aged about 7 years; **Dianne** aged about 2 years; **Matilda** aged about 4 years; **Mary** aged about 38 years; **Sally** aged about 30 years; **Judy** aged about 24 years; **Andrew** aged about 7 years; **Mary** aged about 18 years; **Amy** aged about 20 years; **Jacob** aged about 9[?] years; **Solomen** aged about 6 years; **Rebecca** aged about 16 years; **Ron** aged about 48 years; **Jerry** aged about 4 years; **Sam** aged about 3 years; which negroe Slaves he has brought into this State from the State of South Carolina. 9 January 1843. /s/ D J Smith.

Page 147: Georgia, Camden County. **Joseph Arnow** being sworn saith that he has introduced into this State and County aforesaid from the State of South Carolina a negroe Slave named **Jack** about 14 years of age. 7 June 1843. /s/ Joseph Annw[?].

Page 149: Georgia, Camden County. **Joseph Thomas** being sworn saith[?] that he has introduced into this State from the State of South Carolina **Emily** [illegible]. [Date illegible.] /s/ Joseph Thomas.

Page 151: Georgia, Camden County. **G. Percival Cohen** being sworn saith that he has introduced into the County of Camden aforesaid from the State of South Carolina a female negro Slave named **Tilly** of black complextion aged [blank?] years. [Illegible] April 1847. /s/ [Too faded to read.]

Page 153: **Charles J. Cole** Report of Slaves to be introduced into the State of Georgia: **David** a light complected fellow about 30 years; **Amy** his wife Black negroe about 25 years; **Cinder** about 8 old their child; **little David** about 5 years old their child; **Phebee** black woman about 40 years old; **Ishmael** dark complected about 25; **Jemmy** dark complected about 22 years old; **Clifford** dark complected about 30 years old; **Anatt** dark Complected woman about 24 years old; **Louisa** dark complected woman about 35; **Jacob** dark complected boy about 16 years old; **Ned** dark complected boy about 12 years old; **Adam** dark complected man about 55 years old; **Sharlott** mulatto woman about 50; **Smart** dark complected fellow about 60 years old; **Affy** dark complected woman about 20; **Andrew** dark complected man 24 years old; **Linda** woman dark complected about 22 years old; **Polly** woman dark Complected about 20 years old; **Ben** fellow dark complected about 45 years old; **Clara** mulatto woman about 35 years old; **Arabella** woman mulatto about 23 years old; **Lucinda** woman mulatto about 20 years old; **Casar** boy 16 years old; **Limus** boy about 10 years old; **Peter** light complected man 45 years old; **Nelly** dark complected woman about 30 years old; ~~little~~ **Joe** dark Complected man about 21 years old; **little Peter** boy dark Complected about 5 years old; **Glascow** boy dark complected about 4 years old; **Dick** dark complected man about 30; **Tyra** dark Complected Woman about 28 years old; **Cud Joe** fellow, dark Complected about 18 years old; **Hector** a boy dark Complected years old 14; **Israe** [or Isaac] boy dark complected about 10 years old; **Liddy** girl about 8 years old dark complected; **Mary Ann** woman dark complected 25 years old; **Hager** girl about 8 years old; **Aron** boy black about 5 years old; **Betsy** woman negroe about 20 years old; **Ruben** a light complected fellow about 27 years old; **Hannah** a mulatto about 23 years old; **Andrew** little boy about 4 years old; **little Ben** fellow dark complected about 16 years old; **Jane** child dark complected about 4 years old. Decr 1838.

Page 154: **Wm. Cole. Rachael** dark complected woman age about 25; **Elsy** girl dark complected age about 6; **Ann** girl dark complected about 5. [No date.]

Page 155: Georgia, County of Camden. **Charles J. Cole** formerly of South Carolina being sworn saith that he has introduced into this state the several negroe slaves enumerated and described in the foregoing list with a view to settle and cultivate a plantation Brookfield in the County aforesaid. ~~30th~~ [no other date or signature].

COLUMBIA COUNTY
1818 – 1835

The slave importation register for this county has no title. The original record is in the possession of the Georgia Archives, which has designated it as "Slave Records (Affidavits of people bringing slaves into the State of Georgia.) 1818 – 1835." The microfilm copy is located at the Archives in drawer 48, box 80.

The original volume is unpaginated. All page numbers used herein were assigned by the compiler. Pages 69 and 70 were left entirely blank, and page 24 was left mostly blank.

Many affidavits contain the original signature of the deponent.

In 2007, Mr. David E. Paterson published a version of this register in table format on AfriGeneas (www.afrigeneas.com). Researchers may find great value in his notes on slave importation affidavits in general, and for this county specfically.

Pages 1 – 2: Georgia, Columbia County. **Richard Kennon** of the County of Jasper in said State maketh oath that he is about to introduce into this state two negroes: **Charles** a man slave about 22 years of age, dark complexion, field hand, and **Chloe** a negro girl about fourteen years of age, light complexion and field hand. 20 April 1818. /s/ Rich^d. Kennon.

Pages 2 – 3: Georgia, Columbia County. **Robert Kennon** of said State and County being sworn saith that he is about or intends to introduce into this state a negro girl By name of **Linder** about 12 years of age light complextion, house servant. 21 April 1818. /s/ Robert L Kennon.

Pages 3 – 4: Georgia, Columbia County. **James Lamkin** of said State and County being sworn saith that he is about or intends to introduce into this state a negro boy by the name of **Lewis**, dark complexion about 9 years of age & to be employed as a field hand. 22 April 1818. /s/ James Lamkin.

Pages 5 – 6: Georgia, Columbia County. **William Jones** of said State and County being sworn saith that he is about to introduce a certain girl Slave by the name of **Phillis** thirteen years of age dark complexion & to be employed as a field hand. 6 May 1818. /s/ Wm Jones.

Pages 7 – 8: Georgia, Columbia County. **William Jones** of said State and County being sworn saith that he has introduced a certain girl Slave **Sarah** about twelve years of age, black Complexion and to be employed as a field hand. 5 May 1818. /s/ Wᵐ Jones.

Pages 9 – 10: Georgia, Columbia County. **William Jones** of said State and County being sworn saith that he has introduced a certain girl Slave by the name of **Phillis** thirteen years old, dark complexion and to be employed as a field hand. 7 May 1818. /s/ Wᵐ Jones.

Pages 11 – 14: Georgia, Columbia County. **Samuel Shelly** of said State and County being sworn saith that he is about to introduce into this state a certain girl Slave by the name of **Hannah** thirteen or fourteen years of age, black complexion, and to be employed as a house servant. [No date or signature.]

Pages 15 – 16: Georgia, Columbia County. **James Luke** of the County and State aforesaid being sworn saith that he has introduced into this State certain negro slaves: **Harriot** [later Harriet] eighteen years of age, black complexion, House servant; **Robert** 2 years old, dark complexion; **Aggy**, dark complexion, nine years old, house servant; **Gabriel** six years old, dark complexion; **Absalom** 2 years old, dark complexion; **Esther** twelve years of age, black complexion, field hand; **Hannah**, ten years of age, black complexion, field hand; **Amanda** seven years old, dark complexion, house servant; **Robert** ten years old, dark complexion, field hand; **Henry** eight years of age, dark complexion; **Eliza** nineteen years of age, yellow complexion, field hand. 7 May 1818. /s/ James Luke.

Pages 17 – 18: Georgia, Columbia County. **James Luke** of the County and State aforesaid being sworn saith that he has introduced a certain woman slave by the name of **Violet** twenty five years old, dark complexion field hand. 7 May 1818. /s/ James Luke.

Pages 19 – 22: Georgia, Columbia County. **John Barker** of the County and State aforesaid being sworn saith that he is about to introduce into this State a certain negro slave by the name of **Judy** twenty three years old, black complexion, house servant. 13 May 1818. /s/ John Barker.

Page 23: [Blank except for] /s/ **John Kennon**. Sworn to before me this 8 June 1818 /s/ **A. Crawford**, Clk.

Pages 25 – 27: Georgia, Columbia County. **Hezekiah R. Elgin** of Charles County state of Maryland being sworn saith that he is about to introduce into this state twelve negroes: **Bill**, about 37 years of age dark complexion, field hand; **Rachel** a woman 32 years of age, dark complexion, house servant; **John** a boy 17 years old, black complexion, field hand; **Elly** 14 years old black, field hand; **Hendly**, 14 years old black, field hand; **Judy**, 9 years old, Mullattoe; **Chloe** 7 years old Mullattoe; **Lucinda** 3 years old, Mullattoe; **Thompson** 9 years old dark complexion; **William** 6 years old dark; **Henry** 3 years old, dark complexion; and an

Infant "nameless" and that he is the lawful owner of said slaves, except the above described woman named Rachael and her four children Thompson, William, Henny and an infant as above particularized, which Hezekiah R. Elgin brought from Maryland for **George Cary** a citizen of Columbia County Georgia and to which Cary became intitled to in the State of Maryland aforesaid by reason of intermarriage with his wife **Ann**. 16 July 1818. /s/ Hezekiah R Elgin.

Pages 28 – 29: Georgia, Columbia County. **Jacob Durden** of Jones County in said State being sworn saith that he is about to introduce into this State certain negro slaves: **Moses** about twenty five or twenty seven years of age dark complexion, field hand; **Alick**, about eighteen or twenty years of age, black complexion, field hand; **Alick** a boy about eight or ten years old, dark complexion; **Dorse** about six or eight years old, dark complexion. 28 July 1818. /s/ Jacob W Durden.

Pages 30 – 31: Georgia, Columbia County. **George G. Tankersley** of the County & State being sworn saith that he has introduced a certain negro slave by the name of **Ellis**, about fifteen years old dark Complexion, and a field hand. 14 August 1818. /s/ Geo G Tankersly.

Pages 32 – 33: Georgia, Columbia County. **William Cotton** of the County of Jones and State aforesaid being sworn saith that he is about to introduce into this State a certain negro man by the name of **Mingo**, about 22 years old, dark complexion and a field hand. 24 September 1818. /s/ Wm Cotten.

Pages 34 – 35: Georgia, Columbia County. **Thomas Harden** of the County and State aforesaid being sworn saith that he is about to introduce into this State certain negro slaves: **Easter** about fifteen years of age, dark complexion, field hand; **Lucyann** about Eight years old light complexion. 20 October 1818. /s/ Thomas Harden.

Pages 36 – 37: Georgia, Columbia County. **John Hardin** of the County and State aforesaid being sworn saith that he is about to introduce into this State certain negro slaves: **General**, about 11 years old, black complexion field hand; **Sally** about 35 years old dark complexion field hand; **Mourning** about 3 years old, yellowish complexion. 27 October 1818. /s/ John Harden.

Pages 38 – 39: Georgia, Columbia County. **Josiah Oliver** of the State of North Carolina and Person County being sworn sayith that he is about to introduce into this State certain negro slaves: **Sary** about 22 years of age black complexion, field hand; **Moses** 3 years of age black complexion. 9 November 1818. /s/ Josiah Oliver.

Pages 40 – 41: Georgia, Columbia County. **Verlinda Gardner** of the State and County aforesaid being sworn sayith she is about to introduce into this state certain negro Slaves:

Sary about 22 years of age black complexion a field hand; **Moses** about 3 years of age black complexion. 11 November 1818. /s/ V. Gardner.

Pages 42 – 43: Georgia, Columbia County. **John R. Tullos** of the County and State aforesaid being sworn saith that he is about to introduce into this State a certain negro Slave **Betsey** a woman twenty four years of age, yellow complexion, & a cook. 24 November 1818. /s/ John R Tulloss.

Pages 44 – 45: Georgia, Columbia County. **John P. Bacon** of the County and State aforesaid being sworn saity that he introduced into this State certain negro slaves: **Hasty** a woman about twenty five years old, dark complexion a field hand; **Tony** a negro fellow about 25 years old dark complexion a field hand; **Luke** 12 years old by occupation a field hand; **Jes** a boy about fourteen years of age a field hand. 3 March 1819. /s/ M P Bacon.

Pages 46 – 47: Georgia, Columbia County. **Jordan Prim** of the County and State aforesaid being sworn saith that he is about to introduce into this state a certain negro woman & child, woman by the name of **Duie** 17 years, black complexion & field hand; **child** [not named] three months old, bright complexion. 30 March 1819. /s/ Jordan Prim.

Pages 48 – 49: Georgia, Columbia County. **Edwin Walker** of the county aforesaid being sworn saith that he has introduced into this State: **Jim & Frank** about fourteen years old black complexion field hand; **Henry** about twelve years old dark compliction field hand. 5 April 1819. /s/ Edwin Walker

Pages 50 – 51: Georgia, Columbia County. **Drury B. Fuqua** of the County of Wilkerson Mississippi being sworn saith that he is about to introduce into this State certain negroes: **George** about 33 years of age Field hand dark complexion; **Laborn** about 33 years of age Field hand dark complexion; **Thornton** 20 years of age House Servant Light complexion; **William** 23 years of age Blacksmith with dark complexion; **Sandy** 20 years of age Field hand Dark complexion; **Robert** 18 years of age Field hand Dark complexion; **William** 10 years of age Field hand dark complexion; **Aggy** & child **Aaron** 23 years of age Field hand Light complexion; **Cloe** [later Chloe] 28 years of age dark complexion; **Ary** & child **Eliza** 19 years of age light complexion. 13 April 1819. /s/ D B Fuqua.

Pages 52 – 55: Georgia, Columbia County. **John Foster** of the County & State aforesaid being sworn saith that he is about to introduce into this State certain negroes: **Wake** yellowish complexion a man about 27 years of age, field hand; **Bob** a man, black, about 26 years of age & a field hand; and Peter a man, black, about 20 years of age field hand. 11 March 1820. /s/ J^no Foster.

Pages 56 – 57: Georgia, Columbia County. **Charles G. Gill** of the County & State aforesaid being sworn saith that he has introduced into this state a negro man named **Lawson** about

22 years of age yellow complexion and a house carpenter by trade. 3 January 1821. /s/ Charles G Gill.

Pages 58 – 59: Georgia, Columbia County. **Joel Mayes** of the State of Virginia Greenville County being sworn saith that he is about to introduce into this State certain negro slaves: **Fanny** about 17 years yellow complexion a field hand; **Melinda** about 8 years of age yellow complexion; **Washington** about 7 years of age yellow complexion; **Beck** about 4 years of age yellow complexion. 5 January 1821. /s/ Joel Mayes.

Pages 60 – 61: Georgia, Columbia County. **George W. Hardwick** of the state and county aforesaid being sworn saith that he is about to introduce into this state three certain negro slaves: **Jane** 16 years of age Dark complexion; **Harry** about 14 years of age dark complexion; **Bill** 12 years of age dark complexion. 7 July 1821. /s/ Geo W Hardwick.

Pages 62 – 63: Georgia, Columbia County. **Wᵐ. F. Jackson** agent for **Elizabeth Tankersley** both of said county & state being sworn saith that he has introduced into this state two negroes slaves a negro woman 19 years of age black complexion & named **Mariah**; a boy named **Billy** about thirteen years of age, field hand black complexion. Elizabeth Tankersley for whom he is agent is the lawfull owner of said negroes, slaves. 5 January 1821. /s/ Wᵐ F Jackson – agent of E Tankesley.

Pages 64 – 65: Georgia, Columbia County. **William F. Jackson** agent for **Elizabeth Tankersley** both of said county & state being sworn saith that he has introduced into this state negro slaves: a boy named **Charles** about 13 Years of age of a bright complexion & by profession a plow boy. Elizabeth Tankesley for whom he is agent is the lawfull owner of said Slave. 5 January 1821. /s/ Wᵐ F Jackson agent for E Tankesly.

Pages 66 – 67: Georgia, Columbia County. **Thomas N. Hamilton** of the State & county aforesaid being sworn saith that he is about to introduce into this State certain negro slaves: **Buster** a negro lad 19 years of age black complexion field hand; **Esther** a negro girl 14 years old black complexion; **Hariet** about 10 years old black complexion. 16 February 1822. /s/ Thoˢ N Hamilton.

Page 68: Georgia, Columbia County. **William Redman** of the State & County aforesaid being sworn saith that he is about to introduce into this State a certain negro Slave **Wiley** a lad about 12 or 13 years of age dark complexion. 19 March 1822. /s/ William Redman.

Pages 71 – 72: Georgia, Columbia County. **James Alexander** being sworn saith that he has introduced into this State two certain negro slaves: **Cherry** a Girl about 14 years of age of yellow complexion & **Richard** a boy about 12 yars of age of yellow complexion. 24 January 1831. /s/ J Alexander

Pages 73 – 74: Georgia, Columbia County. **James Pearre** being sworn saith that he has introduced into this state one negro boy slave by the name of **Tom** about 12 years old yellow complexion. 24 January 1831. /s/ James Pearre.

Pages 75 – 76: Georgia, Columbia County. **Richard S. Lazenby** of the County of Warren and State aforesaid being duly sworn saith that he is about to introduce into this state certain negro slaves: **Peter** a boy about 12 years of age dark complexion and **Dave** a boy about ten years of age of dark complexion. 18 February 1831. /s/ Richard S. Lazenby.

Pages 77 – 78: Georgia, Columbia County. **William Hunt** of the County and State aforesaid being sworn saith that he hath introduced into this State Certain negro Slaves: **Lucinda** a woman about 19 years of age dark Complexion house servant; And **Matilda** a woman about seventeen years of age Yellow Complexion house servant. 21 February 1831. /s/ Wᵐ Hunt.

Pages 79 – 80: Georgia, Columbia County. **Benjamin Berry** of the County and State aforesaid being sworn saith that he hath introduced into this State Certain negro slaves: **Sally** a Girl of 13 or 14 years of age of dark complexion; **Mary** a Girl about 8[?] years of age of mulatto complexion. 16 May 1831. /s/ Benjamin Berry.

Pages 81 – 82: Georgia, Columbia County. **Laird Fleming** of the County and State aforesaid being sworn saith that he hath this day as trustee for **Mrs. Mary E. Fleming** introduced into this State a negro woman slave named **Delila** about twenty two years of age of a bright black complexion a House Servant and that he is the lawful owner of said slave as trustee as aforesaid. 4 July 1831. /s/ Laird Fleming.

Pages 83 – 84: Georgia, Columbia County. **Robert Bolton** of the County and State aforesaid being sworn saith that he is about to introduce into this State Certain negro slaves: **Annica** a woman about thirty or thirty five years of age yellow complexion, field hand; also her two children, **Joe** a boy about five years of age of yellow complexion & **Jack** a boy about three years of age of yellow complexion. 3 February 1832. /s/ Robᵗ Bolton.

Pages 85 – 86: Georgia, Columbia County. **Sarah A. Bugg** of the County and State aforesaid being sworn saith that she is about to introduce into this State a negro slave **Anice** a Girl about fourteen years of age of a yellowish Complexion a field hand. 6 February 1832. /s/ Sarah A Bugg.

Pages 87 – 88: Georgia, Columbia County. **James F. Hamilton** of the County and State aforesaid being sworn saith that he is about to introduce into this State a negro slave **Angelina** a woman about Sixteen years of age of yellow complexion a field hand. 6 February 1832. /s/ James F. Hamilton.

Pages 89 – 90: Georgia, Columbia County. **William A. Baldwin** of the county and State aforesaid being sworn saith that he hath introduced into this State a negro boy slave named **Isaac** about fifteen years of age dark complexion & brought up on a farm. 3 November 1832. /s/ Wm A. Baldwin.

Pages 91 – 93: Georgia, Columbia County. **Jeremiah Griffin** of the County and State aforesaid being sworn saith that he hath introduced into this state certain negro slaves: **Mourning** a negro woman & her child **Henry**, Mourning being about twenty years of age of dark complexion and field [*sic*], the child Henry being about 1 year old; **Becky** about 16 years of age dark complexion a field hand; **Tempy** about 14 years of age dark complexion a field hand; **Matilda** about 21 years of age yellow complexion a field hand and her children **Susan** about 6 years, **John** about 4 years & **James** about 2 years of age; **Margaret** about fourteen years of age of yellow complexion a house servant; **Matilda** about twenty years of age dark complexion a field hand and her children **Betsy** 2 years old & **Sally** one year old; **Peggy** about 24 years of yellowish complexion a cook and her two children **Richard** about 7 years old & **Warner** about 2 years old; **Lewis** about 12 years old of yellow complexion a field hand; **Sarah** about 18 years of age of dark complexion a field hand. 18 June 1833. /s/ J Griffin.

Pages 94 – 95: Georgia, Columbia County. **John Lamkin** of the County & State aforesaid being sworn saith that he hath introduced into this State a negro boy slave **Charles** about ten years of age of mulatto Complexion. 6 April 1835. /s/ John Lamkin.

Pages 96 – 97: Georgia, Columbia County. **Peter Wright** of the County and State aforesaid being sworn saith that he hath introduced a negro boy slave **Isaac** of dark Complexion a house servant and Carriage driver about seventeen years of age. 6 April 1835. /s/ Peter Wright.

Pages 98 – 99: Georgia, Columbia County. **Elizabeth J. White** of the County & State aforesaid being sworn saith that she hath introduced into this State three negro slaves: **Kitty** about 17 years old, dark complexion; **Charles** about 16 years old dark complexion; & **Warner** about 15 years old dark complexion; each of them accumstomed to house & out door business. 30 April 1835. /s/ Elizabeth J. White.

Pages 100 – 101: Georgia, Columbia County. **Archibald Heggie** of the County [blank] & State aforesaid being sworn saith that he has introduced into this State a negro Slave **Rachel** a girl about Eleven years old of dark complexion accustomed to nursing & house work. 5 May 1835. /s/ A. Heggie

Pages 102 – 103: Georgia, Columbia County. **Isaac Lucas** of the County and State aforesaid being sworn saith that he hath lately introduced into this State certain negro slaves: **Dave** a negro man about 45 years old of dark complexion a field hand; **William** a boy about 13 years old of yellow complexion no trade; **Tenah** a Girl about 11 years old of dark complexion; **Jane** a Girl about 7 years old of black complexion; **Dave** a boy about 3 or 4 years old black complexion; **Betty** a negro infant child about 6 months old of dark complexion. 13 May 1835. /s/ Isaac Lucas.

ELBERT COUNTY
1822 – 1847

The cover of the book in which affidavits were recorded for Elbert County has only the letter A written on it with the dates 1822 and 1847. There appears to be no other title, except on the spine, which is illegible. The Georgia Archives holds a microfilm copy located in drawer 2, box 76. The film's target sheet gives the following information: Elbert Co., GA, Superior Court, Affidavits for bringing slaves into state, Book A 1822 – 1847.

The clerk skipped page 24 in number. Beginning with page 66, the clerk only numbered the left-hand side of the page, leaving the right-hand side blank and the next left-hand side increasing by 1 rather than 2 page numbers. Right-hand pages are herein referred to by their immediately past left-hand counterpart and the designation [b]. This pagination was continued until page 80, after which each page was numbered sequentially.

Two affidavits were frequently entered into the record on the same page. This volume appears to contain no original signatures for the deponents.

Page 1: Georgia, Elbert County. **Picket Shiflet** being sworn saith that he is about to introduce into this State one negro Slave **Polley** a female Twenty years old dark complexion. 9 July 1822. /s/ Picket Shiflet, his mark "x".

Page 2: Georgia, Elbert County. **Joseph Rucker** being sworn saith that he is about to introduce into this State the following negro Slaves: **Isaac** a male fifteen years old dark complexion; **Robert** a male Six years old dark complexion. 2 July 1822. /s/ Joseph Rucker.

Page 3: Georgia, Elbert County. **Thomas Jones** being sworn saith that he is about to introduce into this State the following negro Slaves: **Hannah** a female twenty seven years old dark complexion and **Patience** a female about one year old dark complexion Common Servants. 18 November 1822. /s/ Thomas Jones.

Page 4: Georgia, Elbert County. **Joseph H. Jones** being sworn saith that he is about to introduce into this State the following negro Slaves: **Easther** a female thirteen years old dark complexion, common Servant. 18 November 1822. /s/ Joseph H. Jones.

Page 5: Georgia, Elbert County. **Parke Blackwell** being sworn saith that he has introduced into this State One Negro Slave **Harriet** thirteen years old dark complexion. 18 January 1823. /s/ Parke Blackwell.

Page 6: Georgia, Elbert County. **Reuben Cleveland** being sworn saith that he is about to introduce into this State one negro slave **Bill** a boy Eleven years old dark complexion Common Servant. 9 October 1822. /s/ Reuben Cleveland.

Page 7: Georgia, Elbert County. **Joseph Rucker** being sworn saith that he has introduced into this State the following negroes Slaves: **Isaac** a male about twelve years old dark complexion and **Billy** a male about twelve years old dark complexion, common Servants. 8 September 1823. /s/ Joseph Rucker.

Page 8: Georgia, Elbert County. **Jeptha V. Harris** being sworn saith that he is about to introduce into this State the following negro Slaves: **Duk** [or Dick] a male twenty two years old and **Robert** a male Twelve years old both dark complexion. 11 February 1824. /s/ J. V. Harris.

Page 9: Georgia, Elbert County. **William Bailey** being sworn saith that he is about to introduce into this State the folllowing negro Slaves: **Rachel** a female seventeen years old dark complexion; **Mariah** a female fifteen years old light complexion, common Servants. 25 October 1824. /s/ William Bailey.

Page 10: Georgia, Elbert County. **Henley Drummond** being sworn saith that he is about to introduce into this State the following negro Slaves: **Henry** a male twenty eight years old, dark complexion; **Dudley** a male twenty four years of age dark; **Dandridge** a male fifteen years old dark complexion; **Amos** a male fifteen years of age dark complexion; **Lewis** a male Eleven years of age dark complexion; **Lucy** a female Eighteen years of age dark complexion; **Salley** a female fifteen years of age dark complexion; **Mary** a female fourteen years of age dark complexion; **Malinda** a female thirteen years of age dark complexion; **Nancy** a female eight years of age dark complexion; **Kitty** a female eight years of age dark complexion; **Pamelia** a female two years of age light complexion; Common servants; that he is the lawful owner of said Slaves, With the exception of two, Henry and Dandridge, of Which he acts as agent. 2 October 1822. /s/ Henley Drummond.

Page 11: Georgia, Elbert County. **James Pledger** being sworn saith that he is about to introduce into this State one negro Slave **Scilla** a female twenty years old dark complexion common Servant. 10 March 1823. /s/ James Pledger.

Page 12: Georgia, Elbert County. **David Dobbs** being sworn saith that he is about to introduce into this State the following negro Slaves: **Hannah** a female twenty Six years old dark complexion; **Tom** a male Six years old dark Complexion; **Adrew** [later Andrew] a male four years old dark complexion; **Silvey** a female two years old dark complexion; and **Caroline** a female three months old dark complexion; common Servants. 23 Mary 1823. /s/ David Dobbs.

Page 13: Georgia, Elbert County. **Richard Ward** being sworn saith that he has introduced into this State **Rachel** a female Sixteen years old light complexion. 3 October 1823. /s/ R. Ward.

Page 14: Georgia, Elbert County. **Robert Hester** being sworn saith that he is about to introduce into this State the following negro Slaves: **Grace** a female twenty nine years old light complexion and her child **George** a male two years old light complexion; **Catharine** a female twenty nine years old dark; **Salley** a female nineteen years old dark; **Lucinda** a female nineteen years old dark; **Julia** a female Sixteen years old dark; **Milly** a female fifteen years old dark; **Sarah** a female twelve years old dark; **Mariah** a female Eleven years old dark; **Scipio** a male Eighteen years old dark; **Sam** a male fifteen years old Mulatto; **Spencer** a male fourteen years old dark; **David** a male twelve years old Mulatto; **Jesse** a male twelve years old dark; **Solomon** a male Eleven years old dark; **Randal** a male nine years old dark; common Servants. 19 November 1823. /s/ Robert Hester.

Page 15: Georgia, Elbert County. **John Dodds** being sworn saith that he is about to introduce into this State one negro Slave a female named **Catharine** four years old dark complexion. 8 July 1822. /s/ John Dodds.

Page 16: Georgia, Elbert County. **Reuben Thornton** being sworn saith that he is about to introduce into this State one negro boy nine years old dark complexion by the name of **Joe**. 25 March 1824. /s/ Reuben his x mark Thornton.

Page 16: Georgia, Elbert County. **Robert Crump** being sworn saith that he is about to introduce into this State one negro boy Slave by the name of **Sandy** about Eleven years of age dark complexion. 11 March 1824. [No signature.]

Page 17: Georgia, Elbert County. **John Davis** being sworn saith that he is about to introduce into this State two Slaves: **Harry** a male Twenty Six years old dark complexion and **Mary** a female twenty three years old dark complexion. 28 April 1824. /s/ John Davis.

Page 18: Georgia, Elbert County. **William Bailey** being sworn saith that he has introduced into this State **Henry** a male twenty one years old dark complexion. 30 December 1823. /s/ William Bailey.

Page 19: Georgia, Elbert County. **Robert N. Diggs** being sworn saith that he is about to introduce into this State the following negro Slaves: **George** a male thirty five years old dark complexion; **Doria** a female twenty four years old light complexion; **Eliza** a female Six years old light complexion; **Emma** a female four years old light complexion; **Ellen** two years old light complexion; **Dolly** Seventeen years old dark complexion; **Thornton** a male Eleven years old light complexion; **Milton** Ten years old dark complexion; **Tenor** a female nine years old dark complexion; common Servants. 8 April 1824. /s/ Robert N. Diggs.

Page 20: Georgia, Elbert County. **Elias Bayless** being sworn saith that he is about to introduce into this State: **Limas** a male forty five years old dark complexion; **Sam** thirty years old dark complexion; **Mason** twenty four years old dark complexion; **Harry** twenty years old dark complexion; **James** Eighteen years old dark complexion; **Edward** Sixteen years old dark complexion; **Trorvin** Sixteen years old dark complexion; **Barnett** twelve years old dark complexion; **Peggy** a female twenty years old dark complexion; **Lucy** Seventeen years old dark complexion; **Mary Jane** Eighteen months old light complexion; **Cenley** a female Seventeen years old light complexion; **Betsey** thirteen years old dark complexion; **Lucy** thirteen years old light complexion; **Jinncy** Eleven years old light complexion; common Servants. 8 April 1831. /s/ Elias Bayless.

Page 21: Georgia, Elbert County. **Beverly Allen** being sworn saith that he has introduced into this State the following negro Slaves: **Ben** a male twenty Six years old, light complexion; **Rachel** a female twenty two years old dark complexion; **Milly** a female about four years old dark complexion; **Alexander** a male eight or nine months months old light complexion. 3 May 1824. [No signature.]

Page 22: Georgia, Elbert County. **Lindsay Johnson** being sworn saith that he is about to introduce into this State the following negro Slaves: **Jack** a fellow twenty five years old dark complexion; **Jane Ann** a female three years old Mulatto. 7 September 1822. /s/ L. Johnson.

Page 22: Georgia, Elbert County. **Archibald Stokes** being sworn saith that he has introduced into this State one negro Slave **Rebecca** a female light complexion about thirteen years old a common Servant. 14 January 1824. /s/ Arch. Stokes.

Page 23: Georgia, Elbert County. **Jeptha V. Harris** being sworn saith that he is about to introduce into this State: **Dick** a male twenty Six years old light complexion; **Silvey** a female twenty five years old light complexion; **Henry** a male eight years old dark complexion; **Addison** a male five years old light complexion; **Chaney** a female dark three years old; & **Phillis** a female eighteen months old light complexion; common Servants. 23 March 1824. /s/ J. V. Harris.

Page 24: Georgia, Elbert County. **Asa Mann** being sworn saith that he is about to introduce into this State **David** a male about thirty years old dark complexion a common Servant. 30 March 1824. /s/ Asa Mann.

Page 25: Georgia, Elbert County. **Nathaniel Banks** being sworn saith that he is about to introduce into this State the following negro Slaves: **Perry** a male about twenty five years old dark complexion; **Dorcas** a female twenty years old light complexion; **Amanda** a female about one year old dark complexion; common Servants. 1 April 1823. /s/ Nathaniel Banks.

Page 25: Georgia, Elbert County. **Jeremiah Horton** being sworn saith that he has introduced into this State one negro Slave **Mary** a female thirteen years old dark complexion. 5 July 1831. /s/ Jeremiah Horton.

Page 26: Georgia, Elbert County. **William W. Bowen** being sworn saith that he has introduced into this State two negro Slaves: **Hetty** a female fourteen years old light complexion and **Austin** a male Eleven years old dark complexion. 9 June 1824. /s/ William W. Bowen.

Page 27: Georgia, Elbert County. **Abner Ward** being sworn saith that he has introduced into this State **William** a male thirteen years old dark complexion a common Servant. 9 June 1824. /s/ Abner Ward.

Page 28: Georgia, Elbert County. **Epps Tucker** being sworn saith that he is about to introduce into this State the following negro Slaves: **Caleb** a male twenty one years old light complexion; **Mina** a female Seventeen years old dark complexion; **Joshua** a male nine years old dark complexion; **Aron** a male ten years old dark complexion; common Servants. 1 June 1824. /s/ Epps Tucker.

Page 29: Georgia, Elbert County. **John Dailey** being sworn saith that he is about to introduce into this State one negro Slave **Ben** thirteen years old dark complexion. 6 November 1823. /s/ John Dailey.

Page 30: Georgia, Elbert County. **John Cleveland** being sworn saith that he is about to introduce into this State: **Ann** a female twenty years old dark complexion; **Eliza** a female three years old dark complexion; **Tom** seven months old dark complexion; common Servants. 17 May 1824. /s/ John Cleveland.

Page 31: Georgia, Elbert County. **James Lockhart** being sworn saith that he is about to introduce into this State one negro Slave **Louisa** a female Eleven years old light complexion. 14 May 1822. /s/ James Lockhart.

Page 32: Georgia, Elbert County. **Arthur C. Atkinson** being duly sworn saith that he is about to introduce into this State the following negro Slaves: **Hab** a male thirty six years old dark complexion and **Suckey** a female thirty years old dark complexion, common Servants. 25 April 1822. /s/ A. C. Atkinson.

Page 32:[1] Georgia, Elbert County. **A. C. Atkinson**, acting as agent in this case for **Grover Howard**, being sworn saith that he is about to introduce into this State a negro Slave **Aderson** a male fifteen years old dark complexion common servant; that as agent aforesaid he is the true and lawful Owner of said Slave. 25 April 1822. /s/ A. C. Atkinson.

Page 33: Georgia, Elbert County. **John Oliver** being sworn saith that he is about to introduce into this State the following negro Slaves: **Amos** a male thirty five years old; **Moses** a male thirty years old; **Arthur** a male seven years old; **Linda** a female twenty three years old; **Edy** a female forty years old; **Jim** a male fourteen years old; **Harriet** a female thirty years old; **Trissy**[?] a female nine years old; **Betsy** a female six years old; **James** a male four years old; **Rachel** a female seventeen years old; **Betsy** a female twenty years old; **Rachel** a female four years old; and **Beverly** a male seven years old; all dark complexion, common slaves. 22 April 1822. /s/ John Oliver.

Page 34: Georgia, Elbert County. **James Reagan** being sworn saith that he is about to introduce into this State the following negro Slaves: **Isaac** a male Eleven years old dark complexion and **Jordan** a male seven years old dark complexion common Servants. 18 February 1822. /s/ James Reagan.

Page 35: Georgia, Elbert County. **Moses Hunt** being sworn saith that he is about to introduce into this State one negro boy Seventeen years old light complexion a Common Servant by the name of **Jack**. 5 April 1824. /s/ Moses Hunt, his mark "x".

Page 36: Georgia, Elbert County. **Thomas Oliver** being sworn saith that he is about to introduce into this State the following negro Slaves: **Nelly** a female twenty three years old dark complexion; **George** a male three years old dark complexion; **Anya** a female Ten months old dark complexion; and **Peter** a male fifteen years old dark complexion; common Servants. 1 May 1822. /s/ Thomas Oliver.

Page 37: Georgia, Elbert County. **Aron A. Yaker** agent for **Benjamin Christler** and **Peter Cloer** being duly sworn saith that he is about to introduce into this State the following negro Slaves: **Milly** a female twenty two years old dark complexion; **Louisa** a female light complexion six years old; and **Polly** a female nineteen months, light complexion; common Servants; that as agent aforesaid he is the true and lawful owner of said Slaves. 25 June 1822. /s/ Aron A. Yager Agt. for Benj[n]. Christler & P. Cloer.

Page 38: Georgia, Elbert County. **Harrison Warren** being sworn saith that he is about to introduce into this State: **James** a male twenty years old dark complexion & **Agness** a female fifteen years old dark complexion common Servants. 1 June 1824. /s/ Harrison Warren.

---

[1] Page number repeated.

Page 38: Georgia, Elbert County. **John McCurry** being sworn saith that he has introduced into this State one negro Slave **Mary** a female Six years old dark complexion common Servant. 5 July 1824. /s/ Jnº. McCurry.

Page 39: Georgia, Elbert County. **Edward Brown** being sworn saith that he is about to introduce into this State **Patty** a female fifteen years old dark complexion. 19 April 1824. /s/ Edward Brown.

Page 39: Georgia, Elbert County. **Thomas Wanslow** being sworn saith that he has introduced into this State **Sarah** a female eight years old dark complexion a common Servant. 10 August 1824. /s/ Thomas Wanslow, his mark "x".

Page 40: Georgia, Elbert County. **John Beck Jnr.** Being sworn saith that he is about to introduce into this State the following negro Slaves: **Jesse** a male 35 years old dark complexion; **Edy** a female 38 years old dark complexion; common Servants. 4 May 1824. /s/ John Beck Jr.

Page 40: Georgia, Elbert County. **John Beck** being sworn saith that he has introduced into this State: **Ben** a male forty years old dark complexion and **Philillis** a female forty years old dark complexion common Servants. 13 July 1824. /s/ John Beck Jnr.

Page 41: Georgia, Elbert County. **Sarah Allman** being sworn saith that she is about to introduce into this State **Caroline** a female thirty years old dark complexion a Common Servant. 10 May 1824. /s/ Sarah Allman, her mark "x".

Page 41: Georgia, Elbert County. **James M. Tait** being sworn saith that he has introduced into this State two negro Slaves: **George** a male about thirty years old dark complexion; **Damon** a male about twenty years old light complexion. 3 April 1824. /s/ Jas M. Tait.

Page 42: Georgia, Elbert County. **Jacob M. Cleveland** being sworn saith that he has introduced into this State: **Jim** a male twenty two years old dark complexion; **Billy** a male nine years old dark complexion; & **Ann** a female sixteen years old dark complexion common Servants. 12 July 1824. /s/ J. M. Cleveland.

Page 42: Georgia, Elbert County. **Reuben Cleveland** being sworn saith that he has introduced into this State **Julia** a female Eleven years old dark complexion a Common Servant. 12 July 1824. /s/ Reuben Cleveland.

Page 43: Georgia, Elbert County. **Reuben Cleveland** being sworn saith that he is about to introduce into this State the following negroes: **Melinda** a female twenty two years old dark complexion & **Mary** a female child five years Old light complexion common Slaves. 27 May 1824. /s/ Reuben Cleveland.

Page 43: Georgia, Elbert County. **Samuel C. Oliver** being sworn saith that he is about to introduce into this State one negro Slave a female Eighteen years old dark complexion by the name of **Lucy**. 20 January 1824. /s/ Saml. C. Oliver.

Page 44: Georgia, Elbert County. **Shelton White** being sworn saith that he has introduced into this State: **Rody** a female twelve years old dark complexion; **Davy** fifteen dark; **Moses** Seventeen dark; **Betsy Jackson** thirteen dark; **Manuel** fourteen dark; **Hannah** eighteen light & her child **Albert Johnson** about Six months old light; **Barbary** fifteen light; **Robin** Eleven dark; **Solomon** Eleven dark; **Salley** ten dark; **Peter** ten dark; **Sam** fifteen light; & **Lewis** eighteen dark; Common Servants. 12 July 1824. /s/ Shelton White.

Page 44: Georgia, Elbert County. **Joseph Rucker** being sworn saith that he has introduced into this State the following negro Slaves: **Jacob** a male 41 years old dark complexion; **Nance** a female 38 years old; **Armsted** a male 7 years old; **Beverly** a male 2 years old; **Selena** a female 17 years old; & **Edmond** "a female" 9 years old; all dark complexion common Servants. 1 June 1824. [No signature.]

Page 45: Georgia, Elbert County. **Jeptha V. Harris** being sworn saith that he has introduced into this State the following negroes: **Bua** a female fourteen years old dark complexion; **Harry** a male Twelve years old dark complexion; **Jefferson** a male Eleven years old dark complexion; and **Henry** a male Ten years old light complexion; Common Servants. [No day or month] 1824. [No signature.]

Page 46: Georgia, Elbert County. **Joseph Rucker** being sorn saith that he has introduced into this State the following negro Slaves: **Davy** a male Seventeen years old light complexion; **Jim** a male nine years old dark complexion; **Cressee** a female Seventeen years old light complexion; **Ally** a female nine years old light complexion; **Cumfort** a female nine years old dark complexion. 20 August 1824. [No signature.]

Page 47: Georgia, Elbert County. **Jesse Rich** being sworn saith that he is about to introduce into this State the following negro Slaves: **Tom** a fellow about twenty Seven years old light complexion; **Susan** a Woman about twenty Six; **Lucinday** a Girl child two years old; **Tom** a male about Ten months old; all light complexion. 22 June 1831. /s/ Jesse Rich.

Page 47: Georgia, Elbert County. **Samuel C. Oliver** being sworn saith that he has introduced into this State the following negro Slaves: **Shadrick** about 13 years old; **Anderson** 13 years; **Olive** about 20 years; **Tillis** 11 years; **Elizabeth** 13 years; **Margaret** 11 years; **Everett** 8 years; **Dicy** 4 years; **Elly** two years; **Amy** 14 years; **Ben** 7 Seven years; **Becky** 14 years; **Hannah** 12 years; **Charles** 16 years; **Mary** 12 years; **Tom** 13 years; **Julia** 7 years; **Olive** 22 years; **Mariah** 18 months; **Crecy** 27 years; **Henry** 18 months; & **Ben** 16 years; all dark complexion. 4 July 1831. /s/ Sam C. Oliver.

Page 48: Georgia, Elbert County. **Hugh McGehee** being sworn saith that he is about to introduce into this State The following negro Slaves: **Malinda** 15 years old; **Ferriba** 14 years old; **Sarah** 12 years old; **Juliett** 22 years old; **Sarah** two years old; **Lettice** 26 years old; **Malinda** two years old; **Clara** 11 years old; **Milly** twenty Six years old; **Jinney** 22 years old; **Mariah**, 19 years old; **Mina** 30 years old; and **Rachel** 26 years old; all dark complexion, except Juliett who is yellow; Common Servants. 5 August 1831. /s/ Hugh McGehee.

Page 49: Georgia, Elbert County. **Nicholas M. Adams** being sworn saith that he is about to introduce into this State one negro boy Slave by the name of **Jeff** about Seven years old dark complexion. 17 April 1830. /s/ Nicholas M. Adams.

Page 50: Georgia, Elbert County. **Benson Maxwell** being sworn saith that he has introduced into this State a negro Woman Slave by the name of **Mariah** and her female Child **Elendor**. Mariah is about twenty years old dark complexion and Eleander is about eight months old dark complexion. 13 April 1830. /s/ Benson Maxwell.

Page 51: Georgia, Elbert County. **Dunston Banks** being sworn saith that he is about to introduce into this State the following negro Slaves: **Dick** a male about thirty five years old yellow complexion; **Jacob** about 30 or 35 dark; **Demsey** about 24 yellow; **Nelson** about 17 mulatto; **Sarah** a female about 16 yellow; **Susan** about 14 yellow; **Mary** about 13 dark; **William** 10 yellow; **Ellick** about 10 dark; **Bob** about 9 dark; **Sam** about 7 yellow; and **Louisa** about 6 yellow; common servants. 8 August 1831. /s/ Dunstan Banks.

Page 52: Georgia, Elbert County. **Joseph Rucker** being sworn saith that he is about to introduce into this State the following Negro Slaves: **Ellick** about ten years old; **Bob** about nine dark complexion; **Sam** about Seven yellow; **Mary** about thirteen years old dark; and **Louisa** about Six years old yellow. 9 August 1831. /s/ Joseph Rucker.

Page 52: Georgia, Elbert County. **Henry Banks** being Sworn saith that he is about to introduce into this State the following Negro Slaves: **Nelson** a Male about Seventeen years old mulatto; **Sarah** a female 16 years old yellow; **Susan** about 14 years old yellow; & **William** about 10 years old yellow; common servants. 9 August 1831. /s/ Henry Banks

Page 53: Georgia, Elbert County. **Bennett Dooly** being Sworn saith that he is about to introduce into this State, a negro boy slave by the name of **Dick**, about nine years of age, dark complexion. 4 October 1831. /s/ Bennet Dooly

Page 53: Georgia, Elbert County. **James Carpenter** being Sworn Saith that he is about to bring into this State the following negro Slaves: **Fanny** a Woman about 27 years old yellow; **Wesley** about Eleven or twelve years old yellow; **Charlotte** about 11 or 12 years old yellow; **Emily** 10 years old yellow; **Bob** about 7 years old yellow; **Boston** about 5 years old yellow; & **Sally** about 2 or 3 years old yellow. 8 October 1831. /s/ James Carpenter.

Page 54: Georgia, Elbert County. **Shelton Oliver** being Sworn saith that he is about to introduce into the State a Negro Slave by the name of **Salley** a Girl about Seventeen years old of yellow Complexion and **Susan** about fourteen years old yellow Complexion. 31 October 1831. /s/ Shelton Oliver.

Page 54: Georgia, Elbert County. **Leroy Upshaw** being Sworn saith that he is about to introduce into this State the following negroe Slaves: **Anderson** a male about thirty five years old Dark complexion; **Lucy** a female about twenty one or two years old, dark Complexion; and **Lexy** a boy about three years old dark Complexion. 11 November 1831. /s/ Leroy Upshaw.

Page 55: Georgia, Elbert County. **George Evenson** being Sworn saith that he is about to introduce into this State the following negro Slaves: **Silvy**, female, 22; **Jincy**, female child, about 5 months; both dark complected. 18 November 1831. /s/ George Eavenson.

Page 55: Georgia, Elbert County. **Ralph Gaines** being sworn saith that he is about to introduce into this State the following negro Slaves: **Charlotte** a female about twenty two years old; & **Mariah** about Sixteen years old; both dark complexion. 19 November 1831. /s/ Ralph Gaines.

Page 56: Georgia, Elbert County. **Bennet Smith** being Sworn saith that he is about to introduce into this State a Negro Slave **Ann** a female about fifteen years of age yellow complexion. 19 November 1831. /s/ Bennet Smith.

Page 56: Georgia, Elbert County. **Josephus Wheelock** being Sworn Saith that he is about to introduce into this State for the purpose of carrying them to the State of Alabama the following negro Slaves: **Fanny** a female about twenty two years old; **Nancy** a female about two years old; & one female **child**, name not known, about two or three months old; all dark complexion. 1 December 1831. /s/ Josephus Wheelock.

Page 57: Georgia, Elbert County. **George Gaines** being Sworn saith that he has introduced into this State the negro Slave **Dave** a male about twelve years old. 9 December 1831. /s/ George Gaines.

Page 57: Georgia, Elbert County. **Elijah Dobbs** being Sworn saith that he is about to introduce into this State the negro Slave **Essen** a male about Eleven years old dark complexion a common servant. 17 January 1832. /s/ Elijah Dobbs.

Page 58: Georgia, Elbert County. **Howell W. Jenkins** being Sworn saith that he is about to introduce into this State the following negro Slaves for the purpose of carrying them to the State of Alabama: **George** a Male about 34 years old dark complexion; **Truy** about Sixteen years old light complexion; **Rebecah** 13 years old dark complexion; **Nelly** 26 dark; **Matilda**

25 years old yellow, & **Child** [not named] 18 months old dark; **Guilford** 25 years old dark; **Lewis** 25 years old yellow; **Charles** 24 years old dark; **Mary** 14 years old yellow; **Eady** 14 years old dark; **Hasty** 13 years old yellow; **Jolly** 15 years old dark; & **Cordelia** 4 years old yellow; Also **Hannah** about Seventeen years yellow; that he is the true and lawful owner of said Slave Hannah.[2] 24 January 1832. /s/ H. W. Jenkins.

Page 59: Georgia, Elbert County. **Humphrey D. Tucker** being Sworn saith that he is about to introduce into this State the following negro Slaves: **Lavina** a Girl about 11 years old yellow complexion; **Payton** a boy about 7 years old yellow; and **Dave** a boy about 5 years old black. 9 March 1832. /s/ H. D. Tucker.

Page 59: Georgia, Elbert County. **Leroy Upshaw** being sworn saith that he is about to introduce into this State a negro Slave **Ben** a boy about Sixteen years of age dark complexion a common servant. 6 April 1832. /s/ Leroy Upshaw.

Page 60: Georgia, Elbert County. **D. W. Hammond** being Sworn Saith that he is about to introduce into this State Eight negroe Slaves: **Juno** a woman about 32 years of age; **Dick** a boy 18 years of age; **Jerry** a boy 9 years old; **Frances** a girl about 10 years old; **William** a boy about 7 years old; **Catharine** about 5 years old; **Fereby** about 3 years old; & **Charles** about 1 year old; all dark complexion; that he is the true and lawful owner of said slaves, with the exception of Frances who belongs to **Alexander Spur** of South Carolina. 24 January 1833. /s/ D. W. Hammond.

Pages 61 – 62: Georgia, Elbert County. **Jeptha V. Harris** being sworn saith that he is about to introduce into this State the following negro slaves: **Sam** a fellow 20 years old dark complexion; **Kitty** a woman 30 years old light; **Thomas** a child 1 year old light; **Nancy** a woman 24 years light; **Francis** a girl 5 old fair; **Susan** a girl 3 years old fair; **Armestead** a boy 1 year; **Levina** a woman 30 years old "rather light complexion"; **Jim** a boy 7 years old dark complexion; **Mary** a girl 3 light; **Walker** a boy 1 dark; ages etc. made out according to the best of deponent's knowledge; all common servants "including Weaver, Spinster, Seamstress, &c." [Blank] day of [blank] 1833. /s/ J V Harris.

Page 63: Georgia, Elbert County. **Jordan Jones** being Sworn saith that he is about to introduce into this State the Negroe Slave **Isaac** a Boy about sixteen years old darke complexion. 20 February 1834. /s/ Jordan Jones.

Page 64: Georgia, Elbert County. **Abnor T. Turman** being Sworn saith that he is about to bring into this state the negro Slave **Precilla** a female about ten years old dark complection. 20 February 1834. /s/ Abnor T. Turman.

---

[2] Information about all but George, Truy, and Hannah recorded in table format.

Page 65: Georgia, Elbert County. **Jacob M. Cleveland** being Sworn saith that he is about to introduce into this State the negroe Slave **Jinny** a female about 48 years old darke complection. 21 May 1834. /s/ Jacob M. Cleveland.

Page 65 – 66: Georgia, Elbert County. **Joseph Rucker** being Sworn Saith that he is about to introduce into this State the following negroe Slaves: **Lewis** a male about fifteen years of age Brown complection and **Joe** a male about 12 years of age Black complection. 19 May 1834. /s/ Joseph Rucker.

Page 66 – 66[b]: Georgia, Elbert County. **Robert Hartness** being sworn saith that he is about to introduce into this State the following negroe Slaves: **Linda** a female about twenty five years old and her **child** [not named] about two years old light complected; **Aggy** a female about fourteen years of age yellow complected; **Harritt** a female about ten years old dark complected; **Balinda** a female about seventeen years of age yellow complected; **Judy** a female about twenty one years of age dark complected; **Eliza** a female about sixteen years of age dark complected; **Eda** a female about thirty years of age dark complected; **Louisa** a female about thirty years old and her **child** [not named] a female about ten months old; **Ester** a female about fourteen years old light complected; **Charles** a male about thirty five years old dark complected a field hand; **Joe** a male about twenty three years old dark complected a field hand; **George** a male about twenty five years old light complected a field hand; **George** a male about fifteen years old dark complected a field hand; **Sam** a male about 30 years old dark complected a field hand; **Jeff** a male about twenty five years old dark complected a field hand. 13 September 1834. /s/ Robt. Hartness.

Page 66[b] – 67: Georgia, Elbert County. **William N. Wyatt** being Sworn saith that he is about to introduce into this State the following Negroe slaves: **Charles** a Male twenty one years of age dark complected a field hand; **Sam** a Male thirteen years of age dark complected a field hand; **Reuben** a Male fourteen years of age black complected a field hand; **Billy** a male thirteen years of age light complected a field hand; **Edmund** a male nine years of age dark complected a field hand; **Elias** a Male about ten years of age dark complected Field hand; **John** a male about two years of age light complected; **Minty** a female about Twenty seven years of age dark complected; **Alla** a Female about eighteen years of age dark complected; **Harrett** a female about twenty one years of age yellow complected; **Mary** a female about eighteen years of age dark complected; **Balinda** a female about fourteen years of age dark complected; **Cotina ann** a female about fourteen years of age dark complected; **Jane** a female about seventeen years of age dark complected; **Ann** a female about six years of age light complected; **Judieth** a female about one year of age. 6 October 1834. /s/ Wm. N Wyatt.

Page 67 – 67[b]: Georgia, Elbert County. **Henry P. Mattox** being Sworn Saith that he is about to introduce into this State the negroe Slave **Dudley** a male about thirtyone years old dark complection. 6 October 1834. /s/ Henry P Mattox.

Pages 67[b] – 68: Georgia, Elbert County. **John Nunnelee** being Sworn saith that he is about to introduce into this State the following negroes Slaves: **Eliza** a female about twenty years of age yellow complexion; **Martha** a female about three years of age yellow complexion; **Katharine** a female about one years of age yellow complected. 9 October 1834. /s/ John Nunnelee.

Page 68: Georgia, Elbert County. **Richmond Rich** being Sworn Saith that he is about to introduce into this State the negroe Slave **Jane** a female about nineteen years of age light complected. 6 October 1834. /s/ R. Rich.

Page 68[b]: Georgia, Elbert County. **Nicholas Burton** being sworn saith that he is about to introduce into this State the negroe Slave **Mary** a female about Eight years of age dark complexion. 9 October 1834. /s/ Nicholas Burton.

Pages 68[b] – 69: Georgia, Elbert County. **Nathen Mattox** being sworn saith that he is about to introduce into this State the Negroe Slave **John** a male about Ten years of age light complected. 9 October 1834. /s/ Nathen Mattox.

Page 69: Georgia, Elbert County. **Bud C. Wall** being sworn saith that he is about to introduce into the State the following Negroe Slaves: **Alice** a female about thirty years of age dark complexion; **Milly** a Female about nine years of age dark complexion; **Sally** a female about Seven years of age dark complexion; **Emila** a female about four years of age dark complexion; **Matilda** a female about one year old dark complexion. 9 October 1834. /s/ Bud C Wall.

Page 69[b]: Georgia, Elbert County. **John Mattox** being sworn Saith that he is about to introduce into this State the following negroe Slaves: **Henry** a male about three years of age yellow complexion; **Fanny** a female about tweny [sic] one years of age yellow. 6 October 1834. /s/ John Mattox.

Pages 69[b] – 70: Georgia, Elbert County. **James M. Henderson** being sworn Saith that he is about to introduce into this State the following negroe Slaves: **Kitt** a Man about twenty two years old dark complexion a field hand; and **Elijah** a boy about Sixteen years old dark complexion a field hand. 13 December 1834. /s/ James M Henderson.

Page 70[b]: Georgia, Elbert County. **William N. Richardson** being Sworn Saith that he is about to introduce into this State the following Negroe Slaves: **Rachel** a female about twenty eight years old "& her two children **Ariana** a female about Six years old _ **Lavinia** three years old all dark complexion." 22 December 1834. /s/ Wm. N. Richardson.

Pages 70[b] – 71: Georgia, Elbert County. **James Patterson** being Sworn Saith that he is about to introduce into this State the following negroe Slaves: **Kitt** a man about twenty two years old dark complexion a field hand; and **Elijah** a Boy about Sixteen years of age dark complexion a field hand. 6 January 1835. /s/ James Patterson.

Pages 71 – 71[b]: Georgia, Elbert County. **John O. Whitfield** being sworn saith that he is about to introduce into this State the following negro Slaves: **Sam** a male about fifty five years old dark complexion a field hand; **Sam** a male about fifty two years old yellow complexion a field hand; **Sam** a male about twenty seven years old yellow complexion a field hand; **Lewis** a Male about thirty eight years old yellow complexion a field hand; **Ben** a male about thirty five years old dark Complexion a field hand; **John** a male about twenty four years of age dark complexion a field hand; **Nat** a male about nineteen years old dark complexion a field hand; **Jarvis** a male about sixteen years old dark complexion a field hand; **Betty**[?] a female about forty eight years old dark complexion a house woman; **Judy** about fourteen years old dark complexion a field hand. 26 January 1835. /s/ John O Whitfield.

Page 71[b]: Georgia, Elbert County. **Benson Maxwell** has this day made an affidavit which describes: **Sam** a male about fifty five years old; **Sam** a male about 52 years old; **Sam** a male about 27 years old; **Lewis** a male about thirtyeight years old; **Ben** a male about thirty five years old; **John** a male about 24 years old; **Nat** a male about 19 years old. Jarvis a male about 16 years old; **Betty** a Female about 48 years old; & **Judy** a female about 14 years old. 26 January 1835.

Pages 71[b] – 72: Georgia, Elbert County. **George Prothro** being Sworn saith that he is about to introduce into this State the Negro Slave **Martha** a Girl about thirteen years old dark complexion. 24 February 1835. /s/ George Prothro.

Page 72[b] – 73: Georgia, Elbert County. **Jonathan Bell** being sworn saith that he is about to introduce into this State the negro Slave **Vina** a Girl about eighteen years old yellow complexion. 7 April 1835. /s/ Jonathan Bell.

Page 73: Georgia, Elbert County. **William Jones** being sworn saith that he is about to introduce into this State the negro Slave **Jim** a boy eighteen years of age rather yellow complexion. 16 March 1835. /s/ William Jones Sr.

Page 73[b]: Georgia, Elbert County. **Joseph Rucker** being sworn saith that he is about to introduce into this State the following Negroes Slaves: **Mary** a Woman about twenty three years of age dark complection; **Billy** a Male about fifteen years of age dark complexion a field hand; **Harritt** a female about twenty seven years of age dark complexion a house woman; **Elmiry** a female about Six years of age yellow complexion; **Mary** a Girl about five years of age yellow complexion; **Dick** a Male about eight years of age dark complexion. 17 June 1835. /s/ Joseph Rucker.

Page 74 – 74[b]: Georgia, Elbert County. **Mark M. Johnson** being sworn saith that he is about to introduce into this State the following Negro Slaves: **Liddy** a woman about twenty five years old dark complexion; **Nelly** a child about two years old dark complection; **Mary** a woman about twenty eight years old dark complexion; **Bill** a Boy about seven years old yellow complexion; **Edwin** a Boy about six years old dark complexion; **Lisha** a Girl about seven years old dark complexion. 21 September 1835. /s/ Mark M Johnson.

Page 74[b]: Georgia, Elbert County. **Philip H. Stifle** being sworn saith that he is about to introduce into this State the following Negro Slaves: **Peter** a Boy about fifteen years old yellow complexion, field hand; **Lora** a female about ten years of age Dark complexion. 2 February 1836. Philip H Stifle.

Page 75: Georgia, Elbert County. **John McCurry** being sworn saith that he is about to introduce into this State the Negro Slave **Jacob** a male about twenty five years of age, dark complexion, a Blacksmith by Trade. 15 February 1836. /s/ John McCurry.

Pages 75[b] – 76: Georgia, Elbert County. **Robert W. Terrell** being sworn saith that he is about to Introduce into this State the following Negro Slaves: **Milly** a woman about twenty five years of age dark complexion; **Martha** a Girl ten years old dark complexion; **Moses** a Boy five years old dark complexion; **Nelson** a Boy about three years old dark complexion; **Wyett** a Boy about 6 months old yellow complexion. 10 June 1836. /s/ R. W. Terrell.

Pages 76 – 76[b]: Georgia, Elbert County. **Henry Cosper** being sworn saith that he is about to introduce into this State the Negro Boy **Peter** about Sixteen years of age, dark complexion, a field hand. 24 January 1837. /s/ Henry Cosper.

Page 77: Georgia, Elbert County. **William Royster** being sworn Saith that he is about to introduce inot this State the Negro Slave **Sceny** a Woman about forty years of age dark complexion a common house woman. 22 March 1837. /s/ Wm. Royster.

Pages 77[b] – 78: Georgia, Elbert County. **John Blakely** being sworn saith that he has introduced into this state for the purpose of carrying into the State of Alabama the following negro slaves: **Will** a man about 35 years old dark; **Daniel** a man about 22 dark; **Ned** a man about 22[?] Light; **Green** a man about 14 dark; **Jacob** a Boy about 9 rather light; **Tom** a Boy about 8 dark; **John** a Boy about 7 dark; **Daver** a Boy about 6 dark; **Hampton** a Boy about 4 dark; **Alfred** a Boy about 6 Mulatto; **Jefferson** a Boy about 3 dark; **Milly** a woman about 30 Light; **Rachel** a girl about 2 dark; **Seller** a girl about 28 dark; **Peter** about 5 months dark; **Lucy** about 18 years dark; **Wingfield** about 5 mo. dark; **Adaline** about 21 years Light; **Nancy** about 23 dark; **Elsey** about 17 dark; **Roxanna** about 23 dark; **Hannah** about 18 dark; **Dilsey** a woman about 15 years old light complex.; **Jinny** a woman about 23 dark; **Julian** a woman about 23 dark; **Hager** a Girl about 12 dark; **Eliza** a Girl about 6 dark; **Creacy** a woman about 26 dark.[3] 21 September 1833. /s/ John Blakely.

Pages 78 – 78[b]: Georgia, Elbert County. **Rufus Haywood** being sworn saith that he has introduced into the State the following negroe Slaves for the purpose of carrying them to Alabama: **Jack** 30 Black; **Mark** 25 Black; **Ben Liles** 25 Black; **Alfred** 27 mulato; **Duke** 40 dark; **Washington** 10 dark; **Dick** 10 dark; **Burrel** 12 dark; **Calvan** 12 dark; **David** 27 dark; **Phil** 20 dark; **Baldwin** 25 dark; **Henry** 24 dark; **Nero** 37 dark; **Peter** 30 dark; **Anderson** 21 dark; **Eliza** 17 dark; **Grizzey** 21 dark; **Rachel** 27 dark; **Martha** nine months; **John** 2 years; **Lucinda** 8 years; **Francis** 2 years; **Hambleton** 4 months; **Rachel Jr.** 5 years.[4] 25 October 1833. /s/ R. Haywood.

Page 78[b]: Georgia, Elbert County. **John M. Raiford** being sworn saith that he introduces into the State the following negroes Slaves: **Louisa**, **Beatrix**, **Willis**, **Luanna**, **Ama** & **Howard**; common Servants; all dark complexion. 9 January 1834. /s/ J. M. Raiford.

Page 79: Georgia, Elbert County. **Richard S. Henderson** being sworn saith that he is about to introduce into this State two negro Slaves: **Horace** a boy five years old; **Uriah** a Boy three years old; each common servants dark complexion. 15 January 1834. /s/ Richard S. his x mark Henderson.

Pages 79 – 79[b]: Georgia, Elbert County. **Joseph Rucker** being Sworn Saith that he has brought, or is about to bring into this State the following negro Slaves: **Joe** a male about twenty three years old, dark complexion; **William** a male about Seven months old, dark complexion; **Gilly** a female about twenty three years old; **Sally** about Seven years old; **Emeline** about Six years old; **Eliza** about two years old; and **Patsey** about thirteen years old; all dark complexion; and **Fanny** about twelve years old yellow complexion; all common Servants. 6 June 1840. /s/ Joseph Rucker.

Page 80: Georgia, Elbert County. **Tinsley W. Rucker** being Sworn saith that he has brought or is about to bring into this State the negro Slave **Simon** a male 28 years old dark complection. 9 April 1844. /s/ T. W. Rucker.

Page 81: Georgia, Elbert County. **John K. Greenway** being Sworn Says that he has brought or is about to bring into this State the negro Slaves named: **Nancey** a female about thirty two years old dark Complexion; and **Milly** a female about ten years old dark Complexion. 12 April 1844. /s/ J W[?] Greenway.

---

[3] Information recorded in table format.
[4] Information recorded in table format.

Page 82: Georgia, Elbert County. **James J. Blackwell** being Sworn Saith that he has brought or is about to bring into thes State the following Negro Slaves: **Bob** a man about twenty Eight years old dark complexion; **Tom** a male about eighteen years of age dark complexion; **Tenor** a female about twenty two years of age yellow complexion; **Edward** a male three years old yellow complexion; **Peggy** a female about twenty two years old dark complexion and her female **child** about a year old "name not known" dark complexion; **Elizabeth** a female about five years old dark complexion; & **Mary** a female three years old dark complexion. 24 February 1844. /s/ Jams J Blackwell.

Page 83: Georgia, Elbert County. **James Lofton** being Sworn Saith that he has brought or is about to bring into the State the following negro Slaves: **Daimon** a male 23 years old dark Complexion; **Siller** a female 18 years old dark Complexion; **Sarah** a female 17 dark Complexion; **Polly** a female 13 dark Complexion; & **Gilphy** a female 11 years old dark Complexion. 1 April 1844. /s/ James Lofton.

Page 84: Georgia, Elbert County. **Isaac Weatherly** being Sworn saith that he has brought or is about to bring into this State the following named Slaves: **Toby** a male 18 years old dark Complexion; **Alfred** a Male 30 years old dark Complexion; **Betsy** a female 18 years old dark Complexion; **Chany** a female 22 years old Light Complexion. 17 May 1844. /s/ Isaac Weatherly.

Page 85: Georgia, Elbert County. **Thomas C. Elliott** Trustee for his Wife **Sarah E. Elliott** being Sworn Saith that he has brought or is about to bring into this State the negro Slave **Rachel** a female Sixteen years old dark Complexion; that he is the true and lawful owner of said Slaves as trustee for his Wife. 4 April 1844. /s/ Thomas C Elliott Trustee for Sarah Elliot.

Page 86: Georgia, Elbert County. **Thomas Cooper White** being Sworn Saith that he has brought or is about to bring into this State the negro Slave **Fredrick** a Male twenty years old dark Complexion. 12 April 1844. /s/ Th. C White.

Page 87: Georgia, Elbert County. **Joseph Rucker** being Sworn Saith that he has brought or is about to bring into this State the following negro Slaves: **John** a Male 18 years old dark Complexion; **Mary** a female 15 years old copper Complexion; **Martha** a female 14 years old dark Complexion. 2 April 1844. /s/ Joseph Rucker.

Page 88: Georgia, Elbert County. **James Carpenter** being sworn saith that he is about to introduce into this State two negroe Slaves: **Martha** a girl about eleven years of age yellow complection; **Irwin** a boy about ten[?] years of age yellow complection. 6 July 1847. /s/ James Carpenter.[5]

---

[5] Recorded in the volume and on a loose sheet of paper apparently tucked into the volume.

The Elbert County, Georgia, affidavit of Reuben Cleveland dated 27th May 1824, stating that he is about to introduce two slaves, Melinda and Mary, into the state. Image source: Elbert County, Georgia, Affidavits for bringing slaves into state, Book A 1822 – 1847: 43; Clerk of the Superior Court, Elberton; Georgia Archives microfilm drawer 2, box 76.

FRANKLIN COUNTY
1818 – 1831

This volume is held by the Georgia Archives. The inside cover reads "Franklin County, Slaves – Importation, 1818 – 1831." The Archives also holds a microfilm copy, located in drawer 200, box 12.

The pages were originally numbered two at a time: the first two pages were page one, the second two pages were page 2, etc., for the first twenty-odd pages. The numbers referred to herein are the small, penciled-in numbers at the bottom of the page, written on odd pages beginning with page 5. The first few pages were blank. Page 34 was also left blank.

The writing in the front half of this volume was very difficult to read due to the ink bleeding through and other damage.

Signatures for some of the deponents may have been original. Many of affidavits recorded in this volume were missing some of the legal language of affidavits taken in other counties.

Pages 4 – 5: Georgia, Franklin County. **Thomas Huson** the following slaves: **Dick** a man of Black complexion about forty five years of age; **Molly** of a yellow complexion about forty years of age; **Poll** a woman of a yellow complexion age forty years; **Crece** of a Black complexion age twenty three; **Fillis** a yellow Girl of Fifteen years of age; **Green** a boy about fifteen years old Black complexion; **Jude** a yallow Girl about nine years of age; **Austen** a boy about Seven years old & yallow; **Hamelton** a boy about three years of age & a yallow complexion; all common field & house hands. 18 January 1818. /s/ Thos Huson.

Pages 6 – 7: Georgia, Franklin County. **Isaac R. Dyche** the following slaves: **Jacob** a man of Dark complexion about twenty five years of age; **Sally** about twenty three years "a woman & her child both of yallow complexion" the Child a girl about seven months of age & by name **Moriah**; **Winne** a girl about Seventeen years of age of a yallow complexion; all common field or house hands. 11 February 1818. /s/ R. Dyche

Pages 8 – 9: Georgia, Franklin County. **Robert Martin** the following slaves: **Sarah** a woman of Black complexion about thirty years of age; **Amy** a Girl of Light complexion about three years of age; **Reuben** a boy of Black complexion about nine years of age; and **Henry** a boy of Black complexion about nine years of age; all common field & house hands. 17 April 1818. /s/ Robert Martin.

Pages 9 – 11: Georgia, Franklin County. **Joseph J. Singleton** the following slaves: **Isaac** a man of Black complection about thirty years of age; **Horace**[?] a man of Black complection about twenty five years of age; **William** about twenty two years of age of Black complection; **Billey** of Black complection about twenty two years of age; **Hector** of Black complection about eighteen years of of age; **Sam** Black Complection about twenty three years of age a carpenter; **Jacob** of Black Complection about twenty three years of age; **Isaiah** of Black Complection about fifteen years of age; **Louisa** a Girl of Black Complection about twenty one years of age; **Absalom** a boy of yellow complection about four years of age; **Sarah** a Girl of Black complection about Eight or nine months old; **Clarinda** a woman of Black complection about thirty years of age; **Castelia** a Boy of Black Complection about forty years of age; **Mariah** a Girl of Black complection about Six months old; **Nancy** a Girl of Black Complection about twenty years of age; **Issibella** a Girl of Black Complection about forty years old; **John** a Boy of Black complection about one year old; **Mary** a Girl of Black Complection about Sixteen years of age; all Common field and house Servants except one Carpenter Sam. 17 June 1818. /s/ J. J. Singleton.

Page 12 – 13: Georgia, Franklin County. **Robert Barnwell** the following slaves: **Grace**[?] a woman of yellow complection about twenty years of age and her son **Charles** of Black complection about two years old; also her son now a **child** of about Six or eight weeks old & not named of Black complection; all common house[?] Slaves. 27[?] June 1818. /s/ Robert Barnwell.

Pages 13 – 15: Georgia, Franklin County. **Charles Sissom**[?] the following Slaves: **Judah** a woman of Black Complection about Seventeen years of age; **Moriah**[?] a Girl of Black Complection about one year old; **Mary** a Girl of Black Complection about thirteen years of age; all common house Servants. 20 June 1818. /s/ Charles Sisson.

Pages 15 – 16: Georgia, Franklin County. **William Simmonds** the following Slaves: **Rach** [later Rachal] a Girl of Black Complection about nineteen years of age; **Mary** a Girl of Black Complection about fifteen years of age; both Common house Servants. 22 June 1818. /s/ Wm Simmonds.

Page 16 – 17: Georgia, Franklin County. **Benjamin Brown** of Elbert County the following Slaves: **Westley** a Boy of Black Complection about Eighteen years of age; **Asberry** a boy of yellow Complection about Sixteen years of age; **Hetty**[?] a Girl of Black Complection about twelve[?] years of age; **Disney**[?] a boy of yellow Complection about nine years of age; all Common field & hosue Servants. 9 September 1818. /s/ B Brown.

Pages 17 – 19: Georgia, Franklin County. **John Hallum** the following Slaves: **William** a man of Dark Complection about twenty two years of age; **Nelson** a man of Dark Complection about eighteen years old; **Lida** a woman of yellow Complection about twenty Six years old; **Harrison** a Boy of Dark Complection about two years old; **Charlotte** a woman a Mulatto about Seventeen years old; **Harriett**, a Mulatto Girl fifteen years old; **Nancy** a woman of Dark Complection Eighteen years old; **Violett** a woman of Dark Complection Nineteen years old; **Rozetah** a mollato[?] Girl thirteen years old; **Scissila** a Girl yellow Complection about ten years old; **Codelea** a Girl yellow Complection nine years old; **Anthoney** a Boy Dark Complection four years old; all common field & house Servants except William a Black Smith. 4 October 1818. /s/ John Hallum.

Pages 19 – 21: Georgia, Franklin County. **Michael McDowell** the following Slaves: two girls named **Nancy** one about Sixteen & the other about Seventeen years of age, both of Dark Complection; **Fanny** a woman about thirty years of age of Dark Complection; **George** a boy about three years of age of Dark Complection; all Common house Servants. 16 November 1818. /s/ M. McDowell[?].

Pages 21 – 22: Georgia, Franklin County. **James Roysten** the following slaves: one Negroe Boy by the name of **Gilbert** about nineteen years of age of Black Complection a Common field Servant. 21 November 1818. /s/ James W. Roysten.

Page 22 – 23: Georgia, Franklin County. **John Payne Senr.** of said County the following Slave about to be interduced into this State by him: a negroe Girl by the name of **Sally** about Eighteen years of age of Dark Complection and a common field or house Servant. 25 November 1818. [No signature.]

Page 24 – 25: Georgia, Franklin County. **Clement Dollar** the Slave **Jack** a Boy about thirteen years of age of Dark Complection a common field Servant. 28 November 1818. /s/ Clement Dollar.

Pages 25 – 26: Georgia, Franklin County. **Thomas Farmer** the following slaves: two Boys one by the name of **Barttlet** about Seven years of age of Black complection; the other by the name of **Tom** about ten years of age of a yallow complection; both common house Servants. 21 March 1820. /s/ Thomas Farmer.

Pages 27 – 28: Georgia, Franklin County. **David R. Sullivan** the following Negroes: **Nub** a woman about twenty five years old of yellow complexion; **Abitha** a Girl about Six years old; **Tom** a boy about three years old; both of dark Complexion. 24 November 1823. /s/ David R Sillavan.

Pages 28 – 30: Georgia, Franklin County. **Bacon Tate** the following slaves: **Betty** a black woman and her child **Milly Ann**; **Jane** a yellow Girl; **Aggy** a Black Girl; **Lucy** dark Complexion; **Jane** a black Girl; **Susan** a Small yellow Girl; all house Servants; **Sam** nineteen years old yellow Complexion; **Billy** nineteen years old dark Complexion; **Fill** fourteen years old dark Complexion; **Hubbard** a black boy Eleven years old; **John** a black boy ten years old; **George** a yellow boy about Eight years old; **Mat** a black boy about Eight years old;

William a yellow boy about fourteen years old; all field hands. 14 May 1824. /s/ Bacon Tate.

Pages 31 – 32: Georgia, Franklin County. **John S. Allen** is about to introduce into this State the following slaves: **Ben** 50 years old Rough shoe maker; **Cato** 50 Blacksmith; **Sarony**[?] 25 Carriage driver; **Nula**[?] 20 Waggoner; **Tom** 40 field hand; **Jeffry** 41 Hewer; **Mick** 26 field hand; **Bill** 24 field hand; **Harry** 21 field hand; **Joe** 21 field hand; **Churcharll** 19 field hand; **Warner** 18 field hand; **Jack** 19 field hand; **George** 12 field hand; **Bobb** 13 field hand; **Horrite** 12 field hand; **Mary** 12 field hand; **Violet** 38 washer &c.; **Drucella** 2; **Mariah** 5[?] field hand; **Dan** 19 field hand; **Wash** 18 field hand; **Ellec** 15 field hand. [6] 25 March 1830. /s/ John S. Allen.

Pages 33: Georgia, Franklin County. **Samuel Nuckols** is about to introduce into this State the three following slaves: **Vurbrage** a man 20 years old Field hand; **Edwin** a man 19 Field hand; **Daroline**[?] a girl 17 Field hand.[7] 16 June 1830. /s/ Samuel Nuckols.

Pages 35 – 36: Georgia, Franklin County. **Dozier Thornton** being duly sworn saith that he and **N. M. Thornton** are about to introduce into this State the following slaves: **Kinchen** a man 37 years old dark complexion; **Jack** a boy 14 yellow; **Daniel** a boy 15 Black; 3 Boys **Jim, Kit & Edmond** from 9 to 11 Black; **Sally** a woman 28 years old dark; her **child** [not named] a boy 8 months old dark; **Sing** [or Siny] a woman 21 years Black; her Child **Elizabeth**[?] 2 months old dark; **Mary** a woman 21 years old dark; her Child **Francis** 8 months old yellow; **Nancy** a woman 21 years old dark; her Child **Henry** 18 months old dark; **Betsy** a girl 14 years old light; **Any** a girl 13 dark; **Nancy** a girl 9 dark; **Betsy** a girl 7 dark; **Juliann** 5 dark; field hands; that he and N. M. Thornton are the lawful owners of said slaves.[8] 6 June 1831. /s/ Dozier Thornton for D & N. M. Thornton.

---

[6] Information recorded in table format.
[7] Information recorded in table format.
[8] Information recorded in table format.

JACKSON COUNTY
1818 – 1830

The original affidavits are located in the back of "Letters of Administration and Guardianship, 1818 – 1843" held by the Probate Court in Jefferson, Jackson Co., GA. The page numbers are taken from the original volume, although the numbers themselves appear to have been added at a much later date.

These affidavits, along with the volume in which they are located, have been microfilmed and are available at the Georgia Archives on microfilm located in drawer 168, box 26. If using the microfilm, these records are located at the front of the record book.

Signatures of the deponents appear to be original and not copies made by the clerk.

Page 275: Georgia, Jackson County. **Charles McKinney Junior** being duly sworn saith that he has brought & introduced into the state & county aforesaid two Negro slaves: a boy by the name of **Edmund**, otherwise Doctor, about fourteen years of age; a Girl about eighteen years of age by the name of **Sall**. Sworn to 5 March 1818. /s/ Ch,s Mckinney Junr.

Page 276: Georgia, Jackson County. **William Park** of this County being duly sworn saith that he has "actually" brought into this State two Negro slaves: one a negro man by the name of **Squire** about twenty two or twenty three years old of a yellowed complexion, a common field Negro; a negro girl named **Aggy** about fourteen years old of black complexion a house girl. Sworn to 25 March 1818. /s/ William Park.

Pages 276 – 277: Georgia, Jackson County. **Stephen Mays** of this County being sworn saith that he has introduced into this State Six negroes: a negro Man named **Andrew** of black complexion about twenty eight years old; A negro woman named **Effey** of black complexion about 15 years old; one girl named **Nancy** of black complexion about 13 years old; **Stephen** a boy of black complexion about ten years in age; **Edy** a woman of black complexion about 27 years old; **Allen** a boy of black complexion about 9 years old which said boy is now at **Mr. Pinsons** in Oglethorpe County as deponant expects. Sworn to 5 May 1818. /s/ Stephen Mayes.

Page 277 – 278: Georgia, Jackson County. **Tandy Key** of said County made oath that he has introduced into this state & County aforesaid nine Negroes: one woman named **Delvy** [or Delcey?] about thirty years of age a black & "her three children **Mema** eight years old, **John** four years old & **Hampton** two years old all black"; one boy named **Daniel** eleven years old; **Harry** nine years old "both black"; one Girl named **Ann** eight years old; **Kelly** seven years old "both black"; **Samuel** about eight years old also black. Sworn to 2 June 1818. /s/ Tandy Key.

Page 278: Georgia, Jackson County. **Robert Martin** of said County being sworn saith that he has introduced into this State & County aforesaid four slaves: **Sary** about thirty years of age of black complexion & her Girl child named **Amy** about three years old of yellow complexion; one boy named **Henry** about nine years old of black complexion; & one boy named **Reuben** about nine years old of black complexion. Sworn to 2 June 1818. /s/ Robert Martin.

Page 279: Georgia, Jackson County. **Doct^r Joseph J. Singleton** being sworn saith that he has introduced into this State & County Eighteen slaves: **Isaac** about 26 [or 36] years old black colour; **Honan**[?] about 24 years old complexion black; **William** about 21[?]; **Billy** about 21; **Hector** about 20; **Sam** about 24 years old "all black"; **Jacob** about 22; **Isaiah** about 15 years old "both black"; **Louisa** about 20, black; **Absalom** a yellow boy, about 4 years old; **Sarah** about 8 months old black; **Clarinda** about 30 years old black; **Castelea**[?] her son black about 4 years old; **Maria** a girl about 8 months old black; **Nancy** about 20 years old black; **Isabella** about 4 years old black; **John** about 1 year old black; **Mary** about 17 years old black. Sworn to 20 June 1818. /s/ Jo^s J. Singleton.

Page 280:   Georgia, Jackson County. **Nathaniel Legg** being sworn saith that he has introduced into this state & County three slaves: one girl named **Kitty** about seventeen years old; two other girls both named **Lucinda** & each about thirteen, all three black complexion. Sworn to 27 June 1818. /s/ Nathl + Legg.

Pages 280 – 281: Georgia, Jackson County. **Green R. Duke** being sworn saith that he has introduced into this state & County one negro boy slave: a boy named **Moses** about nine or ten years old of black complexion. Sworn to 19 March 1819. /s/ Green R Duke.

Page 281: Georgia, Jackson County. **William Montgomery** being sworn saith that he has introduced into this state & County two negro boys Slaves: one a boy named **Wiley** about 14 or 15 years old; the other named **Jesse Franklin** about the same age both of black complexion. Sworn to 17 February 1820. /s/ Wm Montgomery.

Page 282:   Georgia, Jackson County. **Andrew Cunningham** made oath that he has introduced into this state & county one Negro lad named **Joe** about 18 or 19 years old of black complexion. Sworn to 17 February 1820. [No signature.]

Page 283: Georgia, Jackson County. **Jesse Matthews** made oath that he has introduced into this state & county four negroes: **Harry** a Black Negro thirty five years old; **Jenny** a yellow woman nineteen years old; **Isbel** a yellow girl seven; **Hannah** a black girl two years old; the "fellow & wench" field Negroes. Sworn to 3 May 1820. /s/ Jesse Matthews.

Pages 283 – 284:   Georgia, Jackson County. **Randolph Palmer** made oath that he has introduced into this state & county seven negroes: **Silvy** a Negro woman, a Mulatto, about twenty two or three years, & her Children **Alexander** about five years old, **Johnson** about three years old & **Teters** about one year old; one Negro Man named **Adam**, black, about 17 or 18 years old; **Sam**, black, about 12 or 13 years old; & **Stephen** a black boy about 3 or 4 years old; all the grown hands field negroes. Sworn to 4 September 1823. /s/ Randolph Palmer.

Page 284: Georgia, Jackson County. **William D. Martin** being sworn saith that he is about to introduce into this state & county four slaves: one woman named **Mary** aged twenty eight years "inclined to be a Mulatto with tolerable" [remainder not named]. Sworn to [blank] day of [blank] 1830. [No signature.]

The affidavit of Robert Martin dated 2nd June 1818 and filed in Jackson County, Georgia, stating that he had introduced into the state Sary, Amy, Henry, and Reuben. Note the certification by Edward Adams, the Clerk of the Superior Court, at the bottom of the page. Image source: Jackson County, Georgia, Letters of Adminstration and Guardianship, 1818 – 1843: 278; Probate Court, Jefferson; Georgia Archives microfilm drawer 168, box 26.

JASPER COUNTY
1818 – 1832

This volume is located at the Georgia Archives. The volume title is "Record of the oath for Introducing slaves" while the title in the Preliminary Descriptive Inventory at the Archives is "Slave Importation Oaths 1818 – 1832." While the PDI gives the exact title information, the volume is listed under Jasper County, Georgia, Miscellaneous Record Books of the Superior Court, Record Group 179-1-14, Box 1.

This volume is not microfilmed. There is no index to speak of. There are loose records contained within.

Many of the signatures by deponents appear to be original.

Pages 1 – 2: Georgia, Jasper County. **James Pow** on Oath saith that he has introduced into the State and County aforesaid Twelve negro slaves: **Nanny** about Forty years of age; and her child **Rhoda** about Four years of age; **Charles** about Twenty years of age; **Dick** about Eighteen years of age; **Nelly** about sixteen years of age; **Adam** about Fifteen years of age; **Wade** about Eleven years of age; **Anthony** about Eleven years of age; **Taylor** about Eight years of age; **Landy** about Eight years of age; **Lavena** about Twelve years of age; and **Andrew** about Thirteen years of age; all field hands except the Children. 15 January 1818. /s/ James Pow.

Pages 3 – 5: Georgia, Jasper County. **John McQueen** on Oath saith that he has introduced into the State and County aforesaid Twenty two negro Slaves: **June** a fellow supposed to be ~~about~~ Sixty years of age; **Peter** about Forty years of age; **Abram** about Twenty nine years of age; **Ned** about Twenty two years of age; **Murrier** a yellow woman about Thirty Seven years of age; **Isbel** about Thirty five years of age; **Nan** about Twenty seven years of age; **Rhoda** about Twenty five years of age; **Ferriby** about Fourteen years of age; **Frank** a boy about Thirteen years of age; **Shade** about Thirteen years of age; **Viney** a girl about Eight years of age; **Massey** about six years of age; **Abram** a boy about Three years of age; **Julian** a girl about Seven years of age; **Eliza** about Two years of age; **Pheb** about Twelve years of age; **Joe** about four years of age; **Ben** about Eighteen months old; **Rhoda** about Eight years old; **Nancy** about Five years old; and **Rose** about Two years old; all Field hands except the children. 13 February 1818. /s/ John McQueen.[9]

---

[9] This affidavit was also found loose in the back of the book. The loose page appears to have been taken from the current volume or another of similar size.

Pages 5 – 6: Georgia, Jasper County. **Abner Bartlett** on Oath saith that he has introduced into the State and County aforesaid Six negroes: **Louisa** a woman about Twenty five years old; **Cealia** [later Celia] a mulatto girl about Fifteen years old; **Rhody** a woman about Twenty two years old; **Clary** a woman about Twenty eight years old; and her two children, **Lotty** a girl about nine years old and **Thury** a Boy about Eighteen months old; all house Servants except the Child. 6 March 1818. /s/ A Bartlett.

Pages 7 – 8: Georgia, Jasper County. **Thomas Robinson** on Oath saith that he has introduced into the State and County aforesaid Four Negroes: **Polly** a woman about Twenty three years old; **Leah** a girl about sixteen years old; **Garland** a Boy about four years old; and **Sam** about Two years old; the two women considered as field hands. 30 March 1818. /s/ Thomas Robinson.

Pages 8 – 9: Georgia, Jasper County. **Richard Clarke** on Oath saith that he has introduced into the State and County aforesaid Three negroes: **Dowy** a fellow about Thirty ~~years~~ five years old; **Lucy** a woman about Twenty two years old; and **Becky** about Three years old; field hands except the child. 30 March 1818. /s/ Richard Clark.

Pages 10 – 11: Georgia, Jasper County. **Thomas Steen** on Oath saith that he has introduced into the State and county aforesaid one negro boy about seventeen years old by the name of **Sam**, a field hand. 11 April 1818. /s/ Thomas Steen.

Pages 11 – 12: Georgia, Jasper County. **Henry Ware** being sworn saith that he has introduced into the State and County aforesaid one negro fellow named **Solomon** about Twenty seven years old a Blacksmith by trade. 17 April 1818. /s/ Henry Ware.

Pages 12 – 13: Georgia, Jasper County. **James Hodge** on Oath saith that he has introduced into the State and County aforesaid one Negro boy named **Bob** about Twelve years old a field hand. 17 April 1818. /s/ Jas Hodge.

Pages 14 – 15: Georgia, Jasper County. **John H. Marks** on oath saith that he has introduced into the State and County aforesaid Eight negroes: **Charity** a woman about Twenty four years old; **Lezetta** a girl about Five years old; **Vicey** about three years old; **Scillar** about Six months old; **Esther** a girl about Seventeen years old; **Ben** a boy about Ten years old; **Britton** about nine years old; & **Abram** about nine years old; field & house servants except the Children. 3 June 1818. /s/ John H Marks.

Pages 15 – 16: Georgia, Jasper County. **Daniel H. Willis** on Oath saith that he has introduced into the State and County aforesaid Two Negroes: **Izbel** a Woman about Forty five years old; & **Ruth** a girl about Eight years old. July 20, 1818. /s/ Danl. H. Willis.

Pages 16 – 17: Georgia, Jasper County. **Charles Forbes** on oath saith that he has introduced into the State and County aforesaid Two Negro slaves: **Hester** a woman about Twenty four years old a House servant; and **Winney** a Girl about Sixteen years old a field hand. July 27, 1818. /s/ Charles Forbes.

Pages 18 – 19: Georgia, Jasper County. **John R. Cargile** being sworn saith that he has introduced into the aforesaid State and County Six negro Slaves: **Hannah** about sixteen years old; and her child **Sidney** about six months old; **Judy** a girl about Fifteen years old; **Ferriby** about Fourteen years old; **Exom** a Boy about seven years old; and **Charles** about Five years old; all field hands except the Children. 27 August 1818. /s/ John R Cargile.

Pages 19 – 20: Georgia, Jasper County. **Edward Castlebury** on Oath saith that he has introduced into the State and County aforesaid Four Negroes: **Esther** a woman about Twenty five years old; and her Child **Ben** a boy about Three years old; **Arnold** a Boy about Eight years old; & **Caroline** a Girl about Thirteen years old; house & field Servants except the Children. 1 September 1818. /s/ Edward Castleberry.

Pages 20 – 21: Georgia, Jasper County. **John T. Swann** being sworn saith that he has introduced into the State and County aforesaid one Negro girl by the name of **Winney** about Twelve years old, a house servant. 19 September 1818. /s/ John T Swann.

Pages 22 – 23: Georgia, Jasper County. **Mark Ray** on Oath saith that he has introduced into the State and County aforesaid Three negro slaves: **Edwin**, a fellow about Twenty three years old; **Sam**, about Seventeen years old; **Mary** a girl about sixteen years old; all field hands. 6 January 1819. /s/ Mark Ray.

Pages 23 – 24: Georgia, Jasper County. **Mark Ray** on oath saith that he has introduced into this State and County aforesaid one negro slave: **Edmond** a boy about thirteen years of age. 1 December 1819. /s/ Mark Ray.

Pages 24 – 25: Georgia, Jasper County. **John Bogan** on Oath saith that he has introduced into the State and County aforesaid Four Negroes: One Negro fellow named **Jim** about Twenty four years of age a field hand; One Boy named **Dave** about fourteen years old; one boy named **Bill** about Eight years old; and one Girl named **Nancy** about Seventeen years old; all intended as field hands. 5 February 1820. /s/ John Bagan.

Pages 25 – 26: Georgia, Jasper County. **Ethan Stroud** on Oath saith that he has introduced within the limits of the State aforesaid Five negro Slaves: **Fortune** a man about Twenty five years old; **Bill** about ten years old; **Judy** a woman about Twenty eight years old; **Eliza** a girl aobut fourteen years old; and **Peggy** a girl about Twelve years old; all considered as field hands. 7 March 1821. /s/ Ethan Stroud.

Pages 27 – 28: Georgia, Jasper County. **Joseph Sutton** on oath saith that he has introduced into the State and County aforesaid one negro slave: **Mills** about 9 or 10 years of age considered as a field hand. 21 March 1821. /s/ Joseph Sutton.

Pages 28 – 30: Georgia, Jasper County. **James Dowdell** on Oath saith that he has introduced into the State and County aforesaid Twelve negroes Slaves: **Nelson** a fellow about Eighteen years old; **Isaac** about Sixteen years old; **Shadrach** about Seventeen years old; **Lavinia** a girl about Eighteen years old; and her child **Griffen** a boy about Three months old; **Jane** about fifteen years old; **Jess** about Eighteen years old; **Eliza** about Nineteen years old; **Hannah** about Twenty seven years old; **Charlotte** about Seven years old; **Joseph** about nine years old; and **James** about Eight years old; all field hands except the children. 22 ~~July~~ June 1821. Certified June 22, 1821. /s/ James Dowdell.

Pages 30 – 31: Georgia, Jasper County. **Robert Deane** being duly sworn saith that he has introduced into the State & County aforesaid One negro boy by the name of **Bill** about Thirteen years old a field hand. 20 August 1821. /s/ Robert Dean.

Loose record: Tucked between pages 30 and 31 was a loose paper stating the following: "Georgia, Jasper County. Superior Court Clerks Office June 11th 1822. This is to certify that **Samuel Williams** has this day complied with the act of the Legislature of this State relative to the introduction of slaves into this State aforesaid in regard to one negro boy named **Jerry** about Twenty four years old. **John Willson** Clerk." [Emphasis added.]

Pages 31 – 32: Georgia, Jasper County. **John H. Marks** being duly sworn saith that he has introduced into the State and County aforesaid Two Negroes: **Caroline** a girl about Seventeen years old; and **Huldah** a girl about thirteen years old. 23 May 1822. /s/ John H Marks.

Pages 33 – 34: Georgia, Jasper County. **Samuel Williams** on oath saith that he has introduced into this State and County aforesaid one negro by the name of **Jerry** about Twenty four years old a field hand. 11 June 1822. /s/ Samuel Williams.

Page 34: Georgia, Jasper County. "Personally came before me **Lemuel C Laurence** and on oath saith that he has" [nothing further]. [Emphasis added.]

Page 35: Georgia, Jasper County. **William Ware** on oath saith that he has introduced into this State and County aforesaid one negro Boy slave by the name of **Henry** about fourteen years of age. 28 January 1832. /s/ William Ware.

MORGAN COUNTY
1818 – 1824

The original volume where slave importation affidavits were recorded is titled "Trial of Writs of Heabeus Corpus." It is located at the Morgan County Archives in Madison, Georgia. A Criminal Docket dated from 1836 – 1848 was recorded in the back of this volume. A microfilm copy is available at the Georgia Archives in drawer 41, box 48.

No page numbers appear in this volume. The ones used here were assigned by the compiler.

The deponents' signatures appear to be original.

Page 1: Georgia, Morgan County. **Thomas Coleman** being sworn saith that he has interduced into said State (Slaves) who are field hands:. **Mariah**, Fifteen; **Ned**, thirteen; **Cherry**, Ten; **Rachel**, thirteen; and **Aggy**, Fourteen years old. 16 February 1818. /s/ **William Coleman** [*sic*].

Page 2: Georgia, Morgan County. **William Buford** being Sworn Saith that he has Interduced into said State Sixteen Negroes Slaves: **Daniel** a fellow about fifty Seven years old; **Adam**, Forty Six; **Parham**, thirty Six; **Moses**, thirty; **Hall**, twenty three; **Dick**, twenty one; Field hands. **Lawson** a Boy twelve; **Scotland**, Ten; **Isaac**, Nine; **Farny** a Woman Forty Nine; **Delilah**, twenty Six; **Charlotte**, twenty one; **Minny**, Eighteen; **Mary**, Seventeen; **Violet** a Girl, twelve; and **Nelly**, three. 16 February 1818. /s/ William Buford.

Page 3: Georgia, Morgan County. **Samuel McClendon** being Sworn Saith that he has interduced into said State one Negro Man Slave about thirty five years old named **Daniel** a field hand. 28 February 1818. /s/ Samuel McClendon.

Page 4: Georgia, Morgan, County. **Richard Smith** being Sworn Saith that he has interduced into said State a Negroe Woman Slave named **Peggy** about Nineteen years old a house servant. 12 March 1818. /s/ Richard Smith.

Page 5: Georgia, Morgan County. **James Malcom** being Sworn Saith that he has Interduced into said State one Negro Girl Sixteen years of age **Mariah** a field hand. 31 March 1818. /s/ James Malcom.

Page 5: Georgia, Morgan County. **James Malcom Sr.** being sworn saith that he has interduced into said State two negroes (Slaves) Boys one by the name of **Joe** Sixteen years old and the other named **Peter** Seventeen years old both field hands. 31 March 1818. /s/ James Malcom.

Page 6: Georgia, Morgan County. **John Bruster** being Sworn Saith that he has interduced into Said State one Negro Girl twenty three years old named **Charlott** of a yellow complection a field hand. 31 March 1818. /s/John Buster[?].

Page 6: Georgia, Morgan County. **Edmund Adcock** being sworn saith that he has interduced into said State one negro Girl Sixteen years of age named **Taricy** a field hand. 31 March 1818. /s/Edmon Adcock.

Page 7: Georgia, Morgan County. **Earnest C. Wittich** being sworn saith that he is about to interduce into said State a Negro woman named **Keziah** about twenty years of age dark complection and her child named **Robeson** about four months old yellow complection. 9 April 1818. /s/ E C. Wittich

Page 7: Georgia, Morgan County. **Roderick Leonard** being Sworn Saith that he [is] about to interduce into said State a Negro Boy about twelve or thirteen years old named **Peter** Black complection. 9 April 1818. /s/ Rodrick Leonard.

Page 8: Georgia, Morgan County. **James C. Cook** being sworn saith that he has interduced into Said State four Negroes Slaves: a Man Named **Cambridge** yellow complection about Nineteen years old; **Maryan** a Girl about Sixteen years old yellow complection; **Peggy** a Girl about Seven years old yellow complection; & **Joe** a Boy about Eleven years old yellow complection. 10 April 1818. /s/ J. C. Cook.

Page 9: Georgia, Morgan County. **Young Bohannan** being Sowrn Saith the has introduced into said State five negro Slaves: one negro woman 18 years old named **Alzy** dark complexion field hand; **Plilus[?]** a yellow complexion 25 years old field hand; a boy about 12 years old yellow Complexion named **Stephen** field hand; a Small boy named **Charls** about 2 years of age yellow complexion; Small **boy** [not named] about 18 months old dark complexion. 18 April 1818. /s/ Young Bohannan.

Page 10: Georgia, Morgan County. **James Bandy** being Sworn saith he has introduced into said State Three negroes slaves: one boy 20 years of age named **Stephen** field hand; one girl about 20 years of age named **Silva** house girl; one boy child about 13 months old named **Robert**. 22 April 1818. /s/ James Bandy.

Page 10: Georgia, Morgan County. **John L. Moody** being Sworn saith he has introduced into said State five negro Slaves: **Agg** a woman about thirty years of age field hand; **Polly** about

Twelve years of age field hand; **Fanny** about 2 years of age; **Peter** a boy about 14 years old field hand; **Lott** a boy about 13 years of age field hand. 29 April 1818. /s/ Jno. L. Moody.

Page 11: Georgia, Morgan County. **Samuel Fears** being Sworn saith he has interduced into said State two negroes Slaves: one a boy **Moses** 15 years old black complexion field hand; one Girl 14 years named **Paprey [Passrey?]** black complexion house girl. 2 May 1818. /s/ Samuel Fears.

Page 12: Georgia, Morgan County. **Eleazer Jeter** being Sworn Saith he has Interduced into said State Three negro Slaves: one a **Boy** 3 years of age yaler complected [not named]; one negro **woman** 21 years of age yellow complexion field hand [not named]; one negro **woman** 20 years of age dark complexion field hand [not named]. 14 May 1818. /s/ Eleazar Jeter.

Page 13: Georgia, Morgan County. **James Harkness** being sworn saith he has interduced in said State one negro Slaves boy 17 years old named **Silas** field hand dark complexion. 25 June 1818. /s/ James Harkness.

Page 14: Georgia, Morgan County. **Edmond Oniel** being Sworn Saith he is about to interduce into said State one negro man Slave Black Complection about twenty five years of age a field hand named **Charly**. 1 July 1818. /s/ Edmond ONiel, his mark.[10]

Page 15: Georgia, Morgan County. **Samuel Wilder** and **Tobias Holliman** being Sworn saith they has interduced in to said State 9 Negroes Slaves: one woman named **Celia** field hand 30 years of age dark complexion; one boy about eight years old dark complexion anmed **Anson**; one boy about Two years of age named **Hampton** Dark complexion; one boy **Haywood** 6 months old dark complexion; one woman and two children **Mason** 32, **chidren** [*sic*] [not named] 4 years and 1 dark complexion; **Lucenda** a girl 12 years old dark complexion; **Lettis** a girl 12 years old dark complexion; field hands. 13 August 1818. /s/ Samuel Wilder, Tobias Hollimon.

Page 16: Georgia, Morgan County. **Jesse Gun** being Sworn saith he has interduced into said State one negro Slave about Seventeen years old named **Lewis** a field hand. 24 August 1818. /a/ Jesse Gunn.

Page 17: Georgia, Morgan County. **John G. Colbert** being Sworn Saith he has Interduced into said State two negroes Slaves one nam by the name of **Culling** 21 years of age dark; **Jacob** 18 years of age dark complexion; field hands. 25 August 1818. /s/ Jno. G. Colbert.

Page 17 – 18: Georgia, Morgan County. **Joseph Howard** being sworn saith he has Interduced

---

[10] The mark is a capital E turned so that the long line was at the top, parallel to the top of the page, and the "tines" pointed downward.

into said State Three negroes Slaves: one man by the name of **Tony** 45 years of age Dark complexion Field hand; one man by the name of **Jo** 25 years of age Dark Field hand; one girl by the name of **Leah** 14 years of age yellow Complexion. 15 September 1818. /s/ Joseph Howard, his mark "x".

Page 18: Georgia, Morgan County. **Jeremiah Davis** being Sworn Saith he has Interduced in to Said State nineteen negro Slaves: **Peter** a boy 22 years of age Dark complexion field hand; **George** 23 years of age yellow Complexion field hand; **Phillis** a woman 35 years of age dark complexion field hand; **Betsey** a girl 21 years of age yellow complexion; **Molly** 18 years of age dark complexion; **Judy** 11 years old dark complexion; **Lucinda** 9 yellow complexion; **Ann** 7 years of age dark Complexion; **Amy** 7 years old dark; **Nancy** 14 years of age dark complexion; **Jody[?]** 13 years of age yellow complexion; **Peter** 10 years of age dark; **Manuel** 11 years old dark; **Arena** 3 years dark complexion; **David** 18 months old [dark]; **Felita** 3 years lite colour; **Charlott** 18 years old; and child **Peter** 5 years old dark complexion; field hands. 21 September 1818. /s/ Jeremiah Davis.

Page 19: Georgia, Morgan County. **John Morton** being Sworn Saith that he has interduced into said State three Negroes Slaves: **Sikey** about 18 years old of a black complection; **Matilda** about Sixteen years old of a yellow complection; **Nancy** about twelve years old yellow complection; field hands. 24 February 1819. /s/ John Morton.

Page 19: Georgia, Morgan County. **Rober Crawley** [*sic*] being sworn saith that he has intered into said State one negro slave **Barney** about sixteen years of age of a black complection field hand. 13 March 1819. /s/ Robert Crawley.

Page 20: Georgia, Morgan County. **James Watson** being Sworn Saith that he has introduced into Said State Seven Negroes Slaves: **Eliza** a Girl dark complected about thirteen years of age; **Linsey** a girl dark complected about thirteen years of age; **Holland** a girl dark complected about Eleven years of age; **Andrew** a Boy Bleck complected about twelve years of age; **Alfred** a Boy Light complected about twelve years of age; **Warren** a Boy Black complected about twelve years of age; **Littleton** a Boy Black complected about Eight years of age. 19 September 1820. /s/ James Watson.

Page 21: Georgia, Morgan County. **Thomas MaCarton** Agent for **Tenence Cannel** being Sworn Saith that he has interduced as Slaves Eight Negros: **Racheal** a Woman about nineteen years old; **Sylva** a girl about three years of age yellow complected; **England** a boy about one year old dark complected; **Nancy** a woman about twenty five years old; **Elva** a girl about Eight year old; **Scotland** a boy about five year; **Susan** a girl about three year old; **Europe** a boy about 3 months old; that he as agent is the true owner of said Negroes. 29 January 1821. /s/ Thos. McCartan.

Page 22: Georgia, Morgan County. **Stephen H. Gilmire** being Sworn Saith that he has introduced as Slaves five Negroes: **Harry** a lad about Seventeen years of age yellow complected; **Isaac** a boy about Sixteen years old dark complected; **Frederick** a boy about fourteen years old "yellowis" complected; **Jacob** a lad about twelve years of age dark Complected; & **George** a lad about twelve years of age yellowished complected. 27 July 1821. /s/ S. H. Gilmore.

Page 23: Georgia, Morgan County. **Thomas McCarton** being Sworn Saith that he has intered [*sic*] as Slaves Seven Negroes: **Sam** about twenty one yeares of age black Complected; **Emanuel** about twenty two yeares of age black Complected; **Winston** about Seventeen yeares of age black Complected; **Elijah** about Ten years of age; **George** about nine years of age black Complected; **Nancy** about 18 years of Age black; & **Dicy** about Thirteen years of age; all farmers by occupation. 6 August 1821. /s/ Thos. McCartan.

Page 24: Georgia, Morgan County. **Stephen H. Gilmore** being Sworn Saith that he has introduced into the County five Negroes as Slaves: **Easter** a woman about Twenty four years of age; **Rose** a woman about Twenty four years of age; **Hannah** a Girl about Seven years of age; **Anna** a girl about Three years of age; **Mary** a girl about Two months old; all field hands. 19 October 1821. /s/ S. H. Gilmore.

Page 25: Georgia, Morgan County. **Robert Hester** being sworn saith that he has introduced into said County five negroes as Slaves: **Jerry** a man about thirty years of age Black complected; **John** a man about twenty three years old black complected; **Sam** a man about twenty one years of age black complected; **Larkin** a boy about the age of seventeen Molatto Coloured; **Mary** a Girl about the age of sixteen Black Complected. 2 August 1824. /s/ Robert Hester.

On the 18th April 1818, Young Bohannan filed his affidavit in Morgan County, Georgia, attesting that he had introduced into the state Alzy, Plilus[?], Stephen, Charls, and an unnamed boy. Image source: Morgan County, Georgia, Trial of Writs of Habeus Corpus: 9; Morgan County Archives, Madison; Georgia Archives microfilm drawer 41, box 48.

PULASKI COUNTY
1818 - 1820

Affidavits for the importation of slaves may be found at the Georgia Archives on microfilm located in drawer 38, box 46. The target sheet from the film identifies this volume as "Court of Ordinary, Slave Record, 1818 – 1865." There is no title on the book itself.

The affidavits were located on the first sixteen pages of this volume. The remainder of the book is taken up with oaths to not sell spiritous liquors to slaves or free persons of color unless the oath taker is the guardian or owner of said individual.

The scribe assigned page numbers for only the first three pages. Page numbers found thereafter in the following abstracts were assigned by the compiler.

Pages 1 – 2: Georgia, Pulaski County. **George Walker** being sworn saith that he has brought into this State and County as an agent for his father **George Walker Sen**[r]. of said County the following for slaves: **William** a fellow Twenty one years old Black; **Isaac** a boy Sixteen Years old Yellow; **Isom** a boy Twelve Years old Black; **Susan** a woman Twenty three Years old Black. 16 December 1818. /s/ George Walker Jun[r].

Pages 2 – 4: Georgia, Pulaski County. **James M. Taylor** being Sworn saith that he has introduced into this State the following Slaves: **Jim** Twenty one years of age black complected; **George** likely nineteen Years old rather yellow complected; **Jacob**, black pock marked Twenty four years of age; **Ralph** rather yellow complected about twenty five or six years of age; **George** thirty years old rather yellow complected; **Shadrach** Twenty years of age, black; **Dick** Twenty one years of age with a scar on his forehead, rather Yellow; **John**, a tall black fellow about Twenty Seven years of age; which slaves he has introduced as agent for the board of Commissioners for opening and improving the navigation of the Ocmulgee river that the commissioners are the true and lawful owner of said Slaves. 1 February 1819. /s/ Ja[s]. M. Taylor, agent to the Comssr.

Pages 5 – 6: Georgia, Pulaski County. **Allen Tooke** being Sworn saith that he has brought into this State and County for himself and **Arthur Tooke** the following seventeen slaves: **Harry** Forty two; **Ned** twenty one; **Dick** twelve; **Young Harry** eight; **Nelson** four; and **Esther** forty years old; **Jethro** four months old; **Sam** nine years; **Lazrus** nine; **Hulda** Twenty three; **Venus** four; **young Sam** two; **Juda** twenty; and **Rachel** three years old; **Dimcy** fourteen months old; **York** five; and **Young Easter** thirteen years old; all field hands except the Children; that himself and Arthur Tooke are the true and lawful owners of said slaves. 18 February 1819. /s/ Allen Tooke.

Pages 7 – 8: Georgia, Pulaski County. **Allen Tooke** being sworn saith that he has brought into this State and county of Washington as an agent for **Charlotta Tooke**, **Lawrence Tooke**, **Jesse Tooke** and **Allen Tooke** the following two negro slaves **Peggy** eighteen and **Sapha** five years old both field hands and that Charlotta Tooke, Lawrence Tooke, Jesse Tooke and Allen Tooke are the true and lawful owners of said Slaves. 18 February 1819. /s/ Allen Tooke agent.

Pages 8 – 9: Georgia, Pulaski County. **John A. Williams** being sworn saith that he intends and is about to introduce into this State a negro woman Slave of about twenty years of age named **Martha** a house servant, black. 31 May 1819. /s/ J. A. Williams.

Page 10 – 11: Georgia, Pulaski County. **John A. Williams** being sworn saith that he has brought into this State and County one negro woman Slave named **Martha** about twenty years of age house servant. 7 June 1819. /s/ J. A. Williams.

Pages 11 – 13: Georgia, Pulaski County. **Abraham Wood** being sworn saith that he has brought into this State three negro boys: **Lewis**, Black complection about fourteen years of age; **David**, Black about twelve years of age; **Julius Cezar** about ten Years of age Black; all field hands. 17 May 1820. /s/ Abraham Wood.

Pages 13 – 1: Georgia, Pulaski County. **Henry King** being sworn saith that he has introduced into this State the following slaves: **Ishmael** fifty years of age; **Abigail** thirty five Years of age; **Sack** twenty four years of age; all field hands; **Senion** five years of age; **Ishmael** four; & **Abigail** one and a half. December 15, 1820. /s/ H King.

WILKES COUNTY
1818 – 1822

The original volume appears to be titled "Affidavits and Certificates Introducing Slaves into State, Act of the General Assembly Passed 1817, 1818 – 1822." The Georgia Archives has a microfilm copy in drawer 45, box 20.

If using the microfilm, be aware that the film is upside down and backwards.

A very few of the signatures appear to be original to the deponents.

Pages 1 – 2: Georgia, Wilkes County. **Edmond Smith** made oath that he is about to bring into this State four Slaves: **Squire** a Man about Twenty three or four years old; **Lucy** a Girl about fourteen years old; **Isabil** a woman about twenty three years old; and **Ned** a boy about ten years old; all them black complexion. 10 February 1818. /s/ Edmond Smith.

Pages 2 – 3: Georgia, Wilkes County. **Hector Rolls** being Sworn Saith that he is about to introduce in this State Two Slaves: **Joe** a man about thirty five years of age a field hand; **Judia** a woman about twenty one years old a house woman. 24 January 1818. /s/ Hector Rolls.

Pages 3 – 4: Georgia, Wilkes County. **Clemant Billingslea** made Oath that he is about to bring into this State three negro Slaves: **Coalman** a Man about Seventeen or Eighteen years of age; **Betty** a woman a Woman aged about twenty two or three years; and her child **Dulcenia** aged about Eighteen Months old light Complexioned; field slaves. 26 January 1818. /s/ Clement Billingslea.

Pages 4 – 5: Georgia, Wilkes County. **Irbain Lennard** being Sworn Sayith that he is about to introduce in this State Six negro Slaves: **Tom** a man about twenty three years of age a field hand; **Joe** a man about nineteen years of age a field hand; **Sie[?]** a man about twenty three years of age a field hand; **Dick** a man about twenty two years of age a field hand; **Charlott** a Girl about fourteen years of age a house Girl; **Rosetta** a Girl about Seven years of age a house Girl. 10 February 1818. /s/ Irbain Lennard.

Pages 6 – 7: Georgia, Wilkes County. **Martin Moon** being Sworn Syeth that he is about to introduce into this State Six Slaves: **Charles** a Man about thirty yeas of age a field hand; **Nelson** a man about twenty three years of age a field hand; **Bill** a man about twenty three years of age a field hand; **Daniel** a boy about fifteen years of age a field hand; **Bill** a boy about Seventeen years of age a field hand; **Edy** a woman about thirty years of age a house woman. 11 February 1818. /s/ [Illegible mark.]

Pages 7 – 8: Georgia, Wilkes County. **Matthew Mayn** being Sworn Sayeth that he [is] about to bring into this State one Negro Slave named **Anderson** about Eighteen years of age wheel Right Light Complexion. 23 February 1818. /s/ Matthew Mayn.

Pages 8 – 9: Georgia, Wilkes County. **John Robertson Jur.** made oath that he is about to bring into the State of Georgia one Negro girl Slave **Ona** about fourteen years old yellow Complexion a house Girl. 27 February 1818. /s/ John Robertson Jn^r.

Pages 10 – 11: Georgia, Wilkes County. **Francis Billingslea** made oath that he is about to bring into this State four negros: **Charles** a man about thirty four years old yellow Complexion; **Jacob** a Boy Sixteen years old Dark Complexion; **Delpha** a Girl twelve years old light Complexion; **Alsa** a Woman thirty Six years old Dark Complexion. 27 February 1818. [No signature.]

Pages 11 – 12: Georgia, Wilkes County. **James S. Turner** made oath that he is about to bring into this State three negro Slaves: **Prissilla** a woman about thirty two years old; **Tempy** a Girl about Eight years old; **Abram** a boy about six years old of a yellow Complexion; the other two dark. 27 February 1818. /s/Jas. S. Turner.

Page 13: Georgia, Wilkes County. **Abner Dobbs** made oath that he is about to bring into the state of Georgia one negro boy named **Ned** about fourteen years of age dark complexion. 3 March 1818. /s/ Abner Dobbs.

Pages 14 – 15: Georgia, Wilkes County. **John Bird** made oath that he is about to introduce into the State of Georgia five Slaves: A Negro woman named **Jenny** twenty one years of age yellow complexioned a House woman; **Milley** about nineteen years old dark complexioned a field hand; **Dick** a Boy about fourteen years old dark complexioned; **Cosby** a Mulatto Boy about four years old; **Esther** a Girl about ten Months old dark complexioned. 6 March 1818. /s/ John Bird.

Pages 15 – 16: Georgia, Wilkes County. **Thomas McClendon** made oath that he is about to introduce into this State of Georgia Five Slaves: **Fanny** a woman about eighteen years of age dark complected a House woman; **Lucy** a woman about twenty two years of age yellowish complected a House woman; **Dinah** a Girl about twelve years of age yellowish complexion; **Sila** a Girl about Eleven years of age and of yellow complexion; **Jim** a Boy about Eleven years of age of yellow complexion. 25 March 1818. /s/ Thos. McClendon.

Page 17: Georgia, Wilkes County. **Daniel Stone, Esqr.** made oath that he is about to introduce into the State of Georgia four Negro Slaves: **Janny** a woman age twenty years; and her son **Peter** three years old, Dark or black complexion; **Jack** a Boy aged thirteen years Black; **Elsey** a Girl agged Eleven years Black. 31 March 1818. /s/ Daniel Stone.

Pages 18 – 19: Georgia, Wilkes County. **Thomas Persons** made oath that he is about to introduce into the State of Georgia four negroe Slaves: a man by the name of **Tom** about Twenty five or Six years of age of Dark complexion, a Shoemaker; a Boy by the name of **Harry** about fourteen year sof age dark complected; a woman by the name of **Mary** about Seventeen or Eighteen years of age of light complexion; and a Girl **Child** [not named] about three months of age of a light complexion. 11 April 1818. /s/ Thomas Persons.

Pages 19 – 20: Georgia, Wilkes County. **Thomas Gresham** made oath that he has introduced into this State three Negro Slaves: **Isham** a fellow about thirty five years of age dark Complected a Good Cook; **Guy** a boy about ten years of age dark Complected; **Toby** a boy about Nine years of age Dark Complected. 17 April 1818. /s/ Thomas Gresham.

Pages 21 – 22: Georgia, Wilkes County. **Joseph F. Hamblen** made oath that he has introduced into this State of Georgia two Negro Slaves: **Sally** a woman aged about twenty eight years Dark Complection a field hand; and her child **Darcus** about fourteen months. 21 April 1818. /s/ Joseph F. Hamblen.

Pages 22 – 23: Georgia, Wilkes County. **Edward Penick** made Oath that he has introduced into the State of Georgia Six Negro Slaves: **Phillis** a woman about thirty years old yellow Complected field woman; **Jabl** twenty two or three years old black Complection field hand; **Jarrot** a boy about ten or twelve years old yellow Complection; **Jinny** a Girl about Six or Seven years old Dark Complection; **Eliza** a Girl about two or three years old yellowish Complection; **Lewis** a boy about two years old black Complection. 21 April 1818. /s/ Edward Penick, his mark "x".

Pages 23 – 24: Georgia, Wilkes County. **Samuel Fears** Made oath that he has Introduced into the State of Georgia two Negro Slaves: **Moses** a lad about fifteen years of age Black Complection by profession a field hand; **Patsey** about fourteen years of age Black Complection a house girl. 25 April 1818. /s/ Samuel Fear.

Pages 24 – 25: Georgia, Wilkes County. **Thomas J. Morris** Made oath that he has introduced into the State of Georgia two Ngro [sic] Slaves: **Reddick** a man about Sixteen years of ageBlack Complection a field hand; **Drucilla** a Girl about fourteen years of age Black Complection a house Girl. 29 April 1818. /s/ Thomas J. Morris.

Pages 26 – 27: Georgia, Wilkes County. **William S. Stokes** made oath that he has introduced into this State Eight Negro Slaves: **Addam** a Man about Nineteen years of age Black Complection; **Lucy** a Woman about Seventeen years of age; **Letica** a Woman about twenty years of age; **Easter** a Woman about twenty five years of age; **Partrick** a boy about ten year sof age; **Becky** a Woman about twenty four years of age; **Molly** a girl Child about four years old; one boy child by the name of **Washington** about twelve Months of age; all of Black or dark Complection. 4 May 1818. /s/ Wm S Stokes.

Pages 27 – 28: Georgia, Wilkes County. **Gilford Cade** made oath that he is about to Introduce into this State three Negro Slaves: **Asly** a Man about twenty one years of age Complection black a painter by trade; **Betsy** a Woman about Seventeen years of age light Complection a House Woman; **Augustin** a boy about ten or eleven years old Dark. 15 May 1818. /s/ Gilford Cade.

Pages 29 – 30: Georgia, Wilkes County. **Young Stokes Senr.** Made oath that he has introduced into this State Eight Negro Slaves: **Billy** a Man about Nineteen years of age; **Milly** a Woman about twenty two years of age; **Phebe** a Woman about twenty five years of age; **Peggy** a Woman about twenty four years of age; **Louisa** about Ten years of age; a Girl Child **Mary** about Eight years old; and one boy **Harry** about twelve months old; all of Black & Blackish complexion. 4 May 1818. /s/ Young Stokes.

Pages 31 – 32: Georgia, Wilkes County. **Abraham Hill** Made oath that he has introduced into this State three Negro Slaves: **Sigh** a Man about thirty years of age a field hand of Black Complection; **Moses** a boy about Seven or eight years of age Black Complection; **Fanny** a Girl about five years of age yelowish Complection. 5 May 1818. /s/ Abraham Hill.

Pages 32 – 33: Georgia, Wilkes County. **Alfred Wellborn** being Sworn Sayeth that he is about to introduce into the State of Gerogia a Negro Slave Named **Lavina** aged about Seventeen years a Mulatto A House Girl. 5 May 1818. /s/ Alfred Wellborn.

Pages 33 – 34: Georgia, Wilkes County. **James Clay** Made oath that he is about to introduce into the State of Georgia Nine Negro Slaves: **Rachael** a Woman about thirty years of age Black Complection; **Charlott** a Girl about Sixteen years of age yellow Complection; **Lizzy** a Girl about fifteen years old Brown Complection; **Lotty** a Girl fourteen years old Black Complection; **Charity** a Girl Seventeen years old Black Complection; **Phillis** a girl about Eighteen years old Black Complection; **Milly** a Girl thirteen years old Black Complection; **Ussy[?]** a Girl about Seventeen years of age Brown Complection; **John** a boy about five years old yellow Complection. 9 May 1818. /s/ Jo. Clay.

Page 35: Georgia, Wilkes County. **Anslem B. Lee** Made oath that he has introduced into the State of Georgia two Negro Slaves: **Harriet** about Nineteen years of age; & her child **John** three months old; both yellow Complection. 18 May 1818. /s/ Anslem B Leigh.

Pages 36 – 37: Georgia, Wilkes County. **Marshal Martin** Made Oath that he is about to introduce into the State of Ggeorgia three Negro Slaves: **Esther** a Woman fourteen years of age blackish Complection field Girl; **Addam** a boy about fourteen or fifteen years of age yellow Complection field hand; **Loid** a boy about thirteen or fourteen years of age black Complection. 18 May 1818. /s/ Marshall Martin.

Pages 37 – 38: Georgia, Wilkes County. **Joseph Burks** made Oath that he is about to introduce into the State of Georgia A Negro man Slave named **Jim** Nineteen years of Age a black complection a field Slave. 19 May 1818. /s/ Joseph Burks.

Pages 38 – 39: Georgia, Wilkes County. **John Clark** made Oath that he is about to Introduce into the State of Georgia two Negro Boys: **George** a boy about ten years of Age yellow Complection; **Allen** about the Age of ten years Dark Complection. 5 June 1818. /s/ John Clark.

Pages 40 – 41: Georgia, Wilkes County. **Guilford Cade** made oath that he is about to introduce into the State of Georgia the following negro Slaves: **Sam**, twenty one years old, black a field hand; **Simeon** thirty five years old black a field hand; **Joseph** Eleven years old black; **Daniel** nine years old bright complexion; **Dinah** twenty four years old yellow complexion a House Woman; **Sarah** thirty years old of the same complexion as Dinah of same occupation; **Priscilla** fifteen years old of Black complexion a House Girl; **Eliza** twenty nine years old yellow complexion a House Woman; **Louisa** fourteen years old black a House Girl; **Sarah** nine years old, yellow complexion; **Lucy** Ten years of the same Complexion; **Milly** Eleven years of the same complexion; Nancy thirty years old black black; **Hannah** eighteen years old black a House Woman; & her **Child** [not named] two years old black; **Charlotte** Seventeen years old black a House Woman; and her **Child** [not named] Eight months old black; **Zelpha** twelve years old, black a House Girl. 10 June 1818. /s/ Guilford Cade.

Page 42: Georgia, Wilkes County. **Archibald Riddle** made oath that he is about to introduce into the State of Georgia two negro Slaves: **Delpha** a woman twenty years old Dark complexion; **James** a Boy one year old a bright Mulatto. 25 June 1818. /s/ Arch^ld Riddle.

Page 43: Georgia, Wilkes County. **Joseph Wheatley** made oath that he is about to introduce into the State of Georgia the following negro[?] Boy **Billy** about Eleven or twelve years old of dark complexion. 30 June 1818. /s/ Jo^s. Wheatley.

Page 44: Georgia, Wilkes County. **Lewis R. Beaman** made oath that he is about to introduce into the State of Georgia the following negroe Slaves: **Caty** a woman twenty years of age a House Woman dark complexion; & her child **Celina** about thirteen months old a bright Mulattoe. 30 June 1818. /s/ Lewes R Beaman.

Page 45: Georgia, Wilkes County. **Robert Grier** made oath that he is about to introduce into this State the following negroes Slaves: **Milley** twenty eight years old dark complexion;

John Eleven years old dark; **Julian** about six years old dark; **Hillery** a boy about eighteen months old. 2 July 1818. /s/ Robt Grier.

Page 46: Georgia, Wilkes County. **Joseph Key Junr.** Made Oath that he is about to Introduce into this State a Negro Boy Slave **Augusta** Aged Eighteen years black complection. 2 July 1818. /s/ Joseph Key.

Page 47: Georgia, Wilkes County. **Joseph Key Senr.** Made Oath that he is about to Introduce into this State the folowing Negro Slaves: **Sophia** twenty four years old black; **Morioh** a Girl four years old black. 2 July 1818. /s/ Joseph Key Senr.

Page 48: Georgia, Wilkes County. **Thomas Anderson, Esqr.** Made Oath that he has introduced into this State the folowing Negro Slaves: **Demsey** a Negro Boy fifteen years old black Complection; **Chasy** a Girl thirteen years old black Complection; **Ben** a boy Eleven years old yellowish Complection; **Milly** a Girl Nine years old of yellowish[?] Complection. 6 July 1818. /s/ Thos. Anderson.

Page 49: Georgia, Wilkes County. **Nat Burgamy** Made Oath that he has introduced into this State One Negro Slave **Nancy** a Woman about Seventeen years of Age black Complection. 28 July 1818. /s/ Nathl. Burgamy.

Pages 50 – 51: Georgia, Wilkes County. **Archibald Riddle** of said County made Oath that he is about to introduce into the State of Georgia the nine following Negro Slaves: **James** aged twenty seven years old of light complexion a field hand; **James** twenty years old of dark complexion of like occupation; **Daniel** nineteen years old of dark complexion of like occupation; **Archibald** thirteen years old dark complexion; **Charles** Eleven years old dark; **Albert** seven years old dark; **Salley** twenty three years old dark complexion a field hand; **Judah** twenty seven years old dark complexion a field hand; **Mariah** Seven years old dark complexion. 6 August 1818. /s/ Archeb^d. Riddle.

Pages 52 – 53: Georgia, Wilkes County. **Thomas P. Wagnon** made oath that he is about to introduce into the State of Georgia the Six following Negroes Slaves: **John** twenty three years old dark complexion a field hand; **Lewis** Seventeen years old dark complexion of same Occupation; **Glasgow** Seventeen years old Mulattoe of Same Occupation; **Harrison** fourteen years old dark complexion a field hand; **Agnes** Eighteen years old dark complexion a house Woman; **Joanna** fifteen years dark complexion a field hand. 7 August 1818. /s/ Thos. P Wagnon.

Pages 54 – 55: Georgia, Wilkes County. **Wylie Hill** of said County made oath that he is about to introduce into the State of Georgia three negro Slaves: **Judah** a Woman Eighteen years old a bright Mulattoe; **John** a Boy two years old dark complexion; **Dinah** a woman Eighteen years old dark complexion. 25 June 1818. /s/ Wylie Hill.

Pages 55 – 56: Georgia, Wilkes County. **Moses Sutton** Made oath that he is about to introduce into the State of Georgia a Negro boy Slaves Named **Jim** Nineteen Years old dark Complection a field hand. 6 August 1818. /s/ Moses Sutton.

Pages 56 – 57: Georgia, Wilkes County. **William Hamrick** made oath that he is about to introduce into the State of Georgia the Seven folowing Negro Slaves: **Laurence** a Man twenty two years old yellow Complection a field hand; **Nancy** about twenty two years of Age Dark Complection a House Woman; **Susanna** twenty two years of age of yellow Complection a House woman; **Fanny** a Child three years old dark Complection; **Henry** a Child two years old dark Complection; **Mary** a Child three years old Dark; & **Allen** two years old dark Complection. 24 September 1818. /s/ Wm Hammrick[?].

Page 58: Georgia, Wilkes County. **Edward Castleberry** made oath that he is about to introduce into this State four negro Slaves: **Esther** a woman about twenty five years of age dark complexion a House Woman; **Caroline** a Girl about thirteen years of age Dark complexion a House Girl; **Arnold** a Boy about eight years of age dark Complextion; & **Ben** a boy about three years of age Dark complexion. 28 September 1818. /s/ Edward Castleberry.

Page 59: Georgia, Wilkes County. **Richard H. Long** made oath that he has introduced into this State one negro girl by the name of **Alley** about Twelve years of age dark Complected a field hand. 29 September 1818. /s/ Richard H Long.

Page 60: Georgia, Wilkes County. **Purnall Truitt** made oath that he has Introduced into the State of Georgia one negro Slave by the name of **Dave** a man about Twenty Three years of age dark Complection a field hand. 10 October 1818. /s/ Purnall Truitt, his mark "T".

Page 61: Georgia, Wilkes County. **John Cundiff** made Oath that he is about to introduce into this State the following Negro Slaves: **Nancy** a woman about twenty two years old Dark complexion a field hand; **Albert** a Boy about fourteen years old of Dark complexion of the same Occupation. 28 September 1818. /s/ John Cundiff.

Page 62: Georgia, Wilkes County. **Edward Callaway** that he is about to introduce into the State of Georgia the three following negroes Slaves: **Phillis** a woman about twenty one years old, dark Complexion a field [sic]; **Ned** a Boy about two years old; and her small sucking **child** [not named] a girl about 7 weeks old. 13 October 1818. /s/ Edw. Callaway.

Page 63: Georgia, Wilkes County. **John Woolbright** made oath that he has Introduced into this State of Georgia the following negro nman Slave by the name of **Tom** about forty years of Age of dark Complection & a field hand. 3 November 1818. /s/ John Woolbright.

Page 64: Georgia Wilkes County. **Christian Pope** made oath that she has Introduced into this State one negro man Slave about Twenty years of age of a yellow Complexion by the name of **Elijah** a field hand. 25 November 1818. /s/ Christian Pope, her mark "x".

Pages 65 – 66: Georgia, Wilkes County. **Seaton Grantland** one of the Copartners of S. & F. Grantland made Oath that they are about to introduce into this State for the use of the Firm the Six following negroes Slaves: **Hazard** a fellow thirty five years old of light Complexion a field hand; **Isham** thirty five years old black Complexion a Blacksmith; **dick** [*sic*] thirty five years old dark Complexion a rough Carpenter; **Bob** a Boy seven years old black Complexion; **Hannah** a Girl fifteen years old dark a field hand; and **Noah** a Boy nine years old light complexion. 29 October 1818. /s/ Seaton Grantland for S & F Grantland.

Pages 66 – 67: Georgia, Wilkes County. **Seaton Grantland** made oath that he is about to introduce into this State the two following negro Slaves: **Pinky** a Girl about twenty years old Light complexion a House Girl; and **Scott** a fellow about twenty years old a Carriage Driver light Complexion. 29 October 1818. /s/ Seaton Grantland.

Pages 67 – 68: Georgia, Wilkes County. **Henry Pope** of this County made Oath that he is about to introduce into this State the following negro Slaves: **Daniel** a man twenty years Black Complexion a field hand; & **Sally** a woman twenty three years yellow Complexion a field hand. 4 November 1818. /s/ Henry Pope.

Pages 68 – 69: Georgia, Wilkes County. **Andrew Tarver** Made Oath that he ahs introduced into this State three Negro Slaves: **Billy** a Man About twenty two Years of Age Yellow Complection field hand; **Henry** a Man Eighteen Years of Age Dark Complection field hand; **Billy** a Man twenty five Years of Age Black Complection field hand. 15 December 1818. /s/ Andrew Tarver.

Pages 70 – 71: Georgia, Wilkes County. **John Anderson** made oath that he has introduced into this State four Negroes: **Sonnom** a man about twenty five years Old Dark Complected; **Cate** a Woman about thirty five years old yellow complected; **Ama** a Girl Eleven years old yellow Complected; **Edmond** a Child Six Months old yellow Complected; a field hands. 21[?] Decr. 1818. /s/ John Anderson.

Pages 71, 82: Georgia, Wilkes County. **Henry C. Dawson** made Oath that he has Introduced into this State one negro Woman about Twenty Three years of age Dark Complected & House Woman named **Milly**. 27 March 1819. /s/ Henry C Dauson.

Page 72: Georgia, Wilkes County. **Robert Hill** made oath that he has introduced into the State of Georgia the two following negroes Girls Slaves: **Charlotte** thirteen years old yellow complexion; and **Silvy** twelve years old of like Complexion. 22 Decr. 1818. /s/ Robert Hill.

Page 73: Georgia, Wilkes County. **William Edmonds Senr.** made Oath that he has Introduced into this State a Negro Girl Slaves Named **Anna** Sixteen Years Old of yellow

Complection a house Girl. 11 January 1819. /s/ William Wdmond Senr.

Page 74: Georgia, Wilkes County. **Nicholas Wylie** Made Oath that he has introduced into this State of Georgia a Negro Man Slaves Named **Charles** Aged twenty Years of Black Complection a field hand. 15 Decr. 1818. /s/ Nicholas Wylie.

Page 75: Georgia, Wilkes County. **Jesse Slack** Made Oath that he is About to introduce into this State the folowing Negro Slave: **Ben** a Boy Aged Sixteen Black Complection a field hand. 5 January 1819. /s/ Jesse Slack.

Pages 76 – 77: Georgia, Wilkes County. **Alfred Wellborn** Made Oath that he is About to Introduce into this State the four folowing Negro Slaves: **Tenor** a woman twenty two years old of black Complection; **Rose** Nine or ten Years Old a Mulato; **Betsey** Seven years old a Mulatto; **James** four years old Black. 5 January 1819. /s/ Alfred Wellborn.

Pages 77 – 78: Georgia, Wilkes County. **Jack Wilkinson** Made Oath that he has introduced into this State two Negro Slaves: **Milly** a Girl about fifteen years of Age a house Girl; **Sally** a Girl fourteen years of age house Girl; both Yellow Complected. 15 February 1819. /s/ John Wilkinson.

Pages 78 – 79: Georgia, Wilkes County. **Thomas McLuskey** Made Oath that he has Introduced into this State the folowing Negro Slaves: **Moses** a Man about thirty five years of Age a field hand; **Sarrah** a Woman about thirty five years of Age a house Woman; **Wyney** a Woman About twenty Seven years of age a house Woman; **Lucy** a Girl five years of Age; **Wilson** a boy two years of age; **Peter** a Child 6 Months old; all of Dark Complection. 25[?] February 1819. Tho. J. McLeskey.

Page 79: Georgia, Wilkes County. **James Evans** made oath that he has Introduced into this State the following negro Slave girl By the name of **Sally** about eight or nine years of age of Black Complexion. 1 March 1819. /s/ James Evans.

Pages 80 – 81: Georgia, Wilkes County. **Richard H. Long** made Oath that he has introduced into this State one negro Girl by the name of **Alley** about twelve years of age dark Complected a field hand. 29 September 1818. /s/ Richard H Long.

Page 81: Georgia, Wilkes County. **Chenoth Peteet** made oath that he has introduced into this State the following negro Slaves: a Boy by the name of **Gophney** about thirteen years of age and of Black Complexion a plowman; & a **Boy** [not named] about Ten years of age of yellow Complexion. 1 March 1819. /s/ Chenoth Peteet.

Pages 83 – 84: Georgia, Wilkes County. **Hezekiah Salmon** Made Oath that he is about to introduce into this State two Negro Slaves: **Celia** a Woman about Eighteen years of age yellow Complection a field hand; **Phillop** a Boy about thirteen years of age yellow Complection a field hand. 11 June 1819. /s/ Hezekiah Salmon.

Page 84: Georgia, Wilkes County. **Wylie Hill** made oath that he is about to introduce into this State a Negro man Slave named **George** about twenty Six years old, yellow complexion a blacksmith by occupation. 7 October 1819. /s/ Wylie Hill.

Page 85: Georgia, Wilkes County. **Philip Lewis** made oath that he is about to introduce into this State a negro man named **Jacob** about twenty three years of age, of yellow complexion, a field hand & part Blacksmith. 12 June 1820. /s/ Philip Lewis.

Pages 86 – 87: Georgia, Wilkes County. **Phillip Thurman** of Jasper County made oath that he is about to introduce into this state the five following negroe Slaves: **Moody** a boy about nineteen years old of yellowish Complexion; **Violett** his wife sixteen years old of black Complexion; **Hanson** a boy fifteen years old yellow complexion; **Toney** a Boy fifteen years old black Complexion; and **Allen** a Boy twelve years old of black complexion; all field slaves. 29 June 1820. /s/ Phillip Thurmond.

Pages 87 – 88: Georgia, Wilkes County. **Peter Kent** made oath that he is about to introduce into this State a negro woman **Sarah** about seventeen years of Age of black complexion a field Woman. 25 July 1820. /s/ Peter Kent.

Page 89: Georgia, Wilkes County. **James D. Gresham** of this County made oath that he has introduced into this State the following negroes: **Henry** a Boy about twelve years of age Black Complexion a field hand; and **Toney** a Boy about ten years of age Black complexion a field hand. 25 August 1820. /s/ J. D. Gresham.

Pages 90 – 91: Georgia, Wilkes County. **Coleman Williams** made oath that he has introduced into this State the following Negroes: **Robin** a man thirty five years of age Black Complexion a field hand; **Milley** a Woman Eighteen years of age of Black complexion a field hand; **Patsey** twenty two years of age Black complexion a field hand; & her child **Jim** four months old Black complexion; **Fanny** a Girl nine years of age Black complexion a house Girl; & **Jinsy** a Girl Six years old Black complexion a house Girl. 25 August 1820. /s/ Coleman Williams.

Pages 91 – 92: Georgia, Wilkes County. **John Nisbet** made oath that he has introduced into this State the following Negro Slaves: **Jim** a Boy twelve or thirteen years of age of Black complexion; & **Bill** a Boy eleven or twelve years old Black complexion. 8 September 1820. /s/ John Nisbet.

Page 93: Georgia, Wilkes County. **John Norman** made oath that he is about to introduce into this State the following Slave: **Jerry** a lad about nineteen years old of yellow complexion by occupation of field hand. 16 February 1821. /s/ John Norman.

Page 94: Georgia, Wilkes County. **Jesse Norman** made oath that he is about to introduce into this State the following Slave: **George** a boy about thirteen or fourteen years old, a Mulattoe a field boy. 16 February 1821. /s/ Jesse Norman.

Page 95: Georgia, Wilkes County. **Moses Peasley** made oath that he has introduced into this State a Negro Slaves **Moriah**, aged about eighteen years yellow complexion, a field hand. 3 March 1821. /s/ Moses Peasley.

Page 96: Georgia, Wilkes County. **John Dodson** made oath that he is about to introduce into this State the following Negro Slaves: a Negro woman named **Charity** about eighteen years old of Black complexion a house woman; and her child **Peter** eight or nine months old a Mulattoe. 30 April 1821. /s/ John Dodson.

Page 97: Georgia, Wilkes County. **Stovall Pool** made oath that he has introduced into this State the following Negroe Slaves: **Sempy** a woman about eighteen years old lightish complexion a House woman; & **Isaac** a Boy about ten years old black complexion. 8 May 1821. /s/ Stovall Poole.

Page 98: Georgia, Wilkes County. **Thomas D. McLaughlin** made oath that he has introduced into this State the following negroe Slaves: a Negroe named **James** of nutmeg complexion about twenty three years old a field hand; a negro man by the name of **Jerry** of dark complexion about twenty one years of age, a field hand; a negroe Girl named **Salley** of dark complexion about Seventeen years of age, a House Girl. 6 June 1821. /s/ Thos. D. McLaughlin.

Pages 99 – 100: Georgia, Wilkes County. **William Hall** made oath that he is about to introduce into this state the following Negroes Slaves: **Tom** a man about nineteen years of age Dark complexion; & **Stephen** about the same age & same complexion; both field hands. 6 Novr. 1820. /s/ Wm Hall.

Pages 100 – 101: Georgia, Wilkes County. **John H. Broughton** made oath that he is about to Introduce into this state the two following Negro Slaves: **Juda** a girl about fifteen or sixteen years of age Dark complexion field hand; **Esther** a Girl about eight or nine years of age Dark complexion. 7 July 1821. /s/ John H Brougton.

Pages 101 – 102: Georgia, Wilkes County. **John McGehee** made oath that he is about to introduce into this state a negro Woman Slave Eighteen or Nineteen years of age yellow complexion named **Ann**. 19 July 1821. /s/ John S. McGehee.

Pages 103 – 104: Georgia, Wilkes County. **Richard Hingson** made oath that he is about to

Introduce into this state a negro woman Slave Named **Celia** about twelve years of age Dark complexion. 21 February 1821. /s/ Richd Hingson.

Pages 104 – 105: Georgia, Wilkes County. **Burwell Hood** made oath that he has introduced into this State a Negro Girl Slave **Anny** [later Any] about twelve years of age Dark complexion a field hand. 14 March 1821. /s/ Buwell Hood, his mark "x".

Pages 105 – 106: Georgia, Wilkes County. **Byran Shee** made oath that he has introduced into this State the following Negro Slaves: **Dan** a man about 18 years of age Dark complexion a field hand; **Creasy** a woman about 16 years of age Dark complexion a field hand. 11 April 1821. /s/ Byren Shee.

Page 107: Georgia, Wilkes County. **William B. Rotenbury** made oath that he has introduced into this State the following negroe Slaves: **Tom** a man about 30 years of age of dark complexion a field hand; **Dolley** a Girl about fourteen years of age Dark complexion a field hand. 11 April 1821. /s/ W^m B Rottenberry.

Pages 108 – 109: Georgia, Wilkes County. **Green Hull** made Oath that he has introduced into this state the following Negro Slave: **Robin** a man about 60 years of age Dark complexion a field hand; **Jim** a man about 20 years of age Dark complexion a field hand; **Lucy** a woman about 30 years of age Dark complexion a field hand; **Cloe** a woman about 40 years of age Dark a house woman; & her child **Bob** about 2 years of age Dark complexion; **Nancy** a girl about 9 years of age Dark complexion a house girl. 10 April 1821. /s/ Green Hull[?].

Pages 109 – 110: Georgia, Wilkes County. **Daniel Mercer** made oath that he has introduced into this State a Negro woman Named **Amy** of Black complexion twenty three years of age a House woman. 19 May 1821. /s/ Danl. Mercer.

Pages 111 – 112: Georgia, Wilkes County. **David Sayers** made oath that he is about to introduce in to this State the following Negro Slaves: **Willis** a man about twenty four years of age Dark complected a field hand; **Ester** a woman about twenty five years of age Yellow Complected field hand; & her child **Washington** about Ten months of age Yellow complected; **Hardy** a boy about nine years of age Dark complected a field hand. 26 May 1821. /s/ David Sayers.

Pages 113 – 114: Georgia, Wilkes County. **Dudley Pool** made oath that he has introduced into this State a negro Named **Dick** about thirteen years of age Dark Complected a field hand. 4 July 1821. /s/ Dudley Pool, his mark "x".

Pages 114 – 116: Georgia, Wilkes County. **Charles Malone** made oath that he has Introduced into this State the following Negro Slaves: **Lewis** a man about thirty five years of age Dark complexion a field hand; **Nancy** a woman about thirty years of age Dark complexion a house woman; **Rachael** a girl about eight years old Dark complexion; **Emily** a girl about four years of age Dark complection; **Aggy** a Child about six months of age Dark complexion. 2 July 1821. /s/ Charles Malone.

Pages 116 – 117: Georgia, Wilkes County. **Mary Andres** made oath that she has introduced into this state the following Negro slave: **Mary** a Negro girl twelve or thirteen years of age of black complexion a house girl. 3 July 1821. /s/ Mary Andress, her mark "x".

Pages 117 – 119: Georgia, Wilkes County. **George Pullen** made oath that he has introduced into the state of Georgia the following Negro Slave: **Nelly** a woman about sixteen years of age of black complexion a field hand. 3 July 1821. /s/ George Pullen.

Pages 119 – 120: Georgia, Wilkes County. **James W. Gregory** made oath that he has introduced into this State one Negro woman Slave named **Olive** about Seventeen years of age Dark complexion a field hand. 4 July 1821. /s/ James W Gregory.

Pages 121 – 122: Georgia, Wilkes County. **William G. Bowers** made oath that he has introduced into this State the following negroe Slaves: **George** a man about thirty five years old of dark Complexion a field hand; **Jim** a Man twenty Six years of age dark complected a field hand; **Sam** a Man twenty Six years of age of yellow complexion a field [*sic*]; **Ferreby** a Woman thirty five years old dark complected a field hand; **Lindy** a Girl Sixteen years old dark complected; **Barberry** a Girl Sixteen years old yellow complected. 26 September 1821. /s/ Wᵐ G Bowers.

Pages 122 – 123: Georgia, Wilkes County. **John M. Hanson** made oath that he has introduced into this State the following negro Slaves: a negro Woman named **Juda** about twenty one or two years of age of black complexion a field hand; a Girl named **Mary** about eight years of age of yellow complexion; a boy **John** about Six years of age of yellow complexion; **Eliza** a Girl about three or four years of old[?] of yellow complexion; and **Ann** about Eighteen months old of yellow complexion. 10 November 1821. /s/ John M. Hanson.

Pages 123 – 124: Georgia, Wilkes County. **Hezekiah Blankenship** made oath that he is about to introduce into this State the five following Negroe Slaves: **Betty** a woman Seventy or eighty years of age of Black complexion; **Chany** a young woman about eighteen years of age of Black complexion a house Woman; **Phillis** a Girl about thirteen years old of black complexion; **Mary** about nine years old of black complexion; and **bob** [*sic*] a boy about nine years old of black complexion. 30 November 1821. /s/ H Blankenship.

Pages 124 – 125: Georgia, Wilkes County. **Benjamin Stonestreet** after being Sworn Saith that he has introduced into State the following negro Slaves: **Eliza** a woman about nineteen years of age dark complected a house woman; & her child **Harriett** about two years of age dark complected; and **Harriett** a girl about eight years of age dark complected a House girl. 3 December 1821. /s/ Benjamin Stonestreet.

Pages 126 – 127: Georgia, Wilkes County. **Andrew G. Simmes** made oath that he has introduced into the State & County aforesaid the following negro Slaves: **Letty** a woman about fifty five years old of Black complexion; **Arley** thirty five years old black complexion; **Letty** fifteen years old of black complexion; **Tamer[?]** a Girl twelve years old black complexion; **Jinny** nine years old black complexion; **Arley** Six or Seven years old black complexion; **Eliza** a woman above twenty years old of yellow complexion; **Mary** a Girl ten years old of yellow complexion; **Lidda** a woman about twenty years old of black complexion; **Easter** a woman about twenty three years old of black complexion; **Aggy** a girl fourteen or fifteen years old black complexion; **Betty** thriteen to 15 years old black complexion; **Becky** fourteen years old black complexion; **Jemima** a woman about twenty years old of yellowish complexion; **Maria** about twenty one years old of yellow complexion; **Gabriel** A Man twenty Six or twenty Seven years old yellow complexion; **Walker** twenty one to 24 years old black complexion; & **Spencer** a Boy Sixteen or Seventeen years old of black complexion; & **Milly** about 15 years [later a Girl of black complexion]. 15 June 1822. /s/ A. G. Simmes.

Pages 128 – 129: Georgia, Wilkes County. **George Gibson** made oath that he has introduced into this state the following Negro slaves: **Eliza** a Girl about twelve years old black complexion; **Moses** a boy about Eleven Years old black complexion; & **Jack** a boy about Ten Years old black complexion. 22 July 1822. /s/ George Gibson.

SURNAME AND PLACE INDEX

SLAVES [MASTER] INDEX

Some explanation is needed for use of the following index, which contains the names of all slaves mentioned as such in this volume, alphabetized by his or her given name. The names of slave owners or trustees are given in brackets, surname first. In the case that there were two slaves introduced into the state by the same person, an effort was made to distinguish between these individuals by placing his or her age in parentheses after the given name. If no age was given, then another reference might have been used, such as "2nd" (i.e. the second individual of this name in that particular affidavit).

In the rare cases where a slave was mentioned by a given name and a surname, then that individual is indexed here under the given name, and also in the Surname and Place Index under the surname.

Fanny [McClendon, Thomas] 66
Fanny [McDowell, Michael] 47
Fanny [Miller, Robert] 7
Fanny [Moody, John L.] 59
Fanny [Rucker, Joseph] 42
Fanny [Wheelock, Josephus] 36
Fanny [Williams, Coleman] 74
Fanny [Woodruff, Joseph] 5
Farny [Buford, William] 57
Felita [Davis, Jeremiah] 60
Fereby [Hammond, D. W.] 37
Ferreby [Bowers, William G.] 77
Ferriba [McGehee, Hugh] 35
Ferriby [Cargile, John R.] 55
Ferriby [McQueen, John] 53
Fib [Hall, Thomas] 2
Fill [Tate, Bacon] 47
Fillis [Huson, Thomas] 45
Flora [Boisseau, Mary] 7
Flora [Gibson, William] 3, 4
Fortune [Stroud, Ethan] 55
Frances [Robinson, Jane B.] 10
Frances [Spur, Alexander] 37
Francis [Harris, Jeptha V.] 37
Francis [Haywood, Rufus] 42
Francis [Thornton and Thornton] 48
Frank [Bailey, John] 13
Frank [Bailey, William] 9
Frank [McQueen, John] 53
Frank [Robinson, Jane B.] 10
Frank [Walker, Edwin] 22
Franky [DuBose, John W.] 12
Frederick [Gilmore, Stephen H.] 61
Fredrick [White, Thomas Cooper] 43
Friday [Belleme, John] 1
Gabriel [Luke, James] 20
Gabriel [Simmes, Andrew G.] 78
Garland [Robinson, Thomas] 54
General [Hardin, John] 21
George (15) [Hartness, Robert] 38
George (25) [Hartness, Robert] 38
George [Allen, John S.] 48
George [Armstrong, James] 12
George [Atkinson, Mary J. P.] 3, 4
George [Bowers, William G.] 77
George [Clark, John] 69
George [Davis, Jeremiah] 60
George [Diggs, Robert N.] 29
George [Fuqua, Drury B.] 22
George [Gibson, William] 9
George [Gilmore, Stephen H.] 61
George [Hester, Robert] 29
George [Hill, Wylie] 74
George [Jenkins, Howell W.] 36
George [McCartan, Thomas] 61

George [McDowell, Michael] 47
George [Miller, Robert] 7
George [Norman, Jesse] 75
George [Oliver, Thomas] 32
George [Tait, James M.] 33
George [Tate, Bacon] 47
George [Taylor, James M.] 63
George [Woodruff, Joseph] 5
Georgie [Robinson, Jane B.] 10
Gilbert [Roysten, James] 47
Gilly [Rucker, Joseph] 42
Gilphy [Lofton, James] 43
Glascow [Cole, Charles J.] 16, 18
Glasgow [Wagnon, Thomas P.] 70
Glass [Hickman, Joshua] 2
Gophney [Peteet, Chenoth] 73
Grace [Hester, Robert] 29
Grace [Smith, James M.] 15
Grace[?] [Barnwell, Robert] 46
Green [Blakely, John] 41
Green [Huson, Thomas] 45
Griffen [Dowdell, James] 56
Grizzey [Haywood, Rufus] 42
Guilford [Jenkins, Howell W.] 37
Guy [Gresham, Thomas] 67
Hab [Atkinson, Arthur C.] 31
Hager [Blakely, John] 42
Hager [Cole, Charles J.] 17, 18
Hager [Hall, Thomas] 2
Hager [Smith, James M.] 15
Hall [Buford, William] 57
Hambleton [Haywood, Rufus] 42
Hamelton [Huson, Thomas] 45
Hampton [Bailey, William] 9
Hampton [Blakely, John] 41
Hampton [Key, Tandy] 50
Hampton [Wilder and Holliman] 59
Hannah [Blakely, John] 41
Hannah [Cade, Guilford] 69
Hannah [Cargile, John R.] 55
Hannah [Cole, Charles J.] 17, 18
Hannah [Dobbs, David] 28
Hannah [Dowdell, James] 56
Hannah [Gilmore, Stephen H.] 61
Hannah [Hall, Thomas] 2
Hannah [Hickman, Joshua] 2
Hannah [Jenkins, Howell W.] 37
Hannah [Jones, Thomas] 27
Hannah [King, James] 8
Hannah [Lang, Richard] 14
Hannah [Luke, James] 20
Hannah [Matthews, Jesse] 51
Hannah [Oliver, Samuel C.] 34
Hannah [S. & F. Grantland] 72
Hannah [Shelly, Samuel] 20

Jim [Nisbet, John]...74
Jim [Oliver, John]..32
Jim [Rucker, Joseph]...34
Jim [Smith, James M.]..15
Jim [Sutton, Moses]...71
Jim [Taylor, James M.].......................................63
Jim [Thomas, George W.].....................................14
Jim [Thornton and Thornton]...............................48
Jim [Walker, Edwin]...22
Jim [Williams, Coleman]......................................74
Jimmy [Cole, Charles J.].....................................16
Jimy [Smith, James M.].......................................15
Jincy [Evenson, George]......................................36
Jingo [Smith, James M.]......................................15
Jinncy [Bayless, Elias].......................................30
Jinney [DuBose, John W.].....................................12
Jinney [Hickman, Joshua].......................................2
Jinney [McGehee, Hugh].......................................35
Jinny [Blakely, John]...41
Jinny [Cleveland, Jacob M.]..................................38
Jinny [Gibson, William]...9
Jinny [Hall, Thomas]...2
Jinny [Penick, Edward]..67
Jinny [Simmes, Andrew G.]....................................78
Jinsy [Williams, Coleman]....................................74
Jo [Howard, Joseph]...60
Joanna [Wagnon, Thomas P.]...................................70
Jody[?] [Davis, Jeremiah].....................................60
Joe (little) [Cole, Charles J.]...............................18
Joe [Allen, John S.]..48
Joe [Bachtoll, Alexander].....................................13
Joe [Belleme, John]..1
Joe [Bolton, Robert]..24
Joe [Chevalier, John]..7
Joe [Clark, Archibald].......................................2, 4
Joe [Clark, Samuel]...10
Joe [Clarke, Samuel]..10
Joe [Cole, Charles J.]..16
Joe [Cook, James C.]..58
Joe [Cunningham, Andrew]......................................50
Joe [Gibson, William]...6
Joe [Hall, Thomas]...2
Joe [Hartness, Robert]..38
Joe [Lennard, Irbain]...65
Joe [Malcom, James Sr.].......................................58
Joe [McQueen, John]...53
Joe [Rolls, Hector]...65
Joe [Rucker, Joseph].......................................38, 42
Joe [Smith, David John].......................................17
Joe [Thornton, Reuben]..29
Joe [Woodruff, Joseph]..5
John (1st) [Robinson, Jane B.]................................10
John (2nd) [Robinson, Jane B.]................................10
John [Blakely, John]..41
John [Cary, George]...20

John [Clarke, Samuel]...12
John [Clay, James]..68
John [Desclaux, Joseph]..6
John [Descloux, Joseph]..6
John [Grier, Robert]..70
John [Griffin, Jeremiah]......................................25
John [Hall, Thomas]..2
John [Hanson, John M.]..77
John [Haywood, Rufus]...42
John [Hester, Robert]...61
John [Hill, Wylie]..70
John [Key, Tandy]...49
John [Leigh, Anslem B.].......................................68
John [Mattox, Nathen]...39
John [Maxwell, Benson]..40
John [McKendree, William].....................................13
John [Rucker, Joseph]...43
John [Singleton, Dr. Joseph J.]...............................50
John [Singleton, Joseph J.]...................................46
John [Tate, Bacon]..47
John [Taylor, James M.].......................................63
John [Wagnon, Thomas P.]......................................70
John [Whitfield, John O.].....................................40
John [Wyatt, William N.].....................................38
Johnson [Palmer, Randolph]....................................51
Jolly [Jenkins, Howell W.]....................................37
Jonathan [Woodruff, Joseph]....................................5
Jordan [Reagan, James]..32
Jorden [Robinson, Jane B.]....................................10
Joseph [Cade, Guilford].......................................69
Joseph [Dowdell, James].......................................56
Josey [Smith, James M.].......................................15
Joshua [Tucker, Epps]...31
Juckolad[?] [Smith, James M.].................................15
Juda [Brougton, John H.]......................................75
Juda [Hanson, John M.]..77
Juda [Tooke and Tooke].......................................63
Judah [Hill, Wylie]...70
Judah [Riddle, Archibald].....................................70
Judah [Sisson, Charles].......................................46
Jude [Huson, Thomas]..45
Judia [Rolls, Hector]...65
Judieth [Wyatt, William N.]...................................38
Judy [Barker, John]...20
Judy [Cargile, John R.].......................................55
Judy [Cary, George]...20
Judy [Davis, Jeremiah]..60
Judy [Hartness, Robert].......................................38
Judy [Maxwell, Benson]..40
Judy [Smith, David John]......................................17
Judy [Stroud, Ethan]..55
Judy [Whitfield, John O.].....................................40
Julia [Cleveland, Reuben].....................................33
Julia [Hester, Robert]..29
Julia [Oliver, Samuel C.].....................................34

Salley [White, Shelton] 34
Sally [Berry, Benjamin] 24
Sally [Carpenter, James] 35
Sally [Cole, William D.] 17
Sally [Dyche, Isaac R.] 45
Sally [Evans, James] 73
Sally [Griffin, Jeremiah] 25
Sally [Hamblen, Joseph F.] 67
Sally [Hardin, John] 21
Sally [Payne, John Senr.] 47
Sally [Pope, Henry] 72
Sally [Rucker, Joseph] 42
Sally [Smith, David John] 17
Sally [Thornton and Thornton] 48
Sally [Wall, Bud C.] 39
Sally [Wilkinson, Jack] 73
Sally [Woodruff, Joseph] 5
Sam (27) [Maxwell, Benson] 40
Sam (27) [Whitfield, John O.] 40
Sam (52) [Maxwell, Benson] 40
Sam (52) [Whitfield, John O.] 40
Sam (55) [Maxwell, Benson] 40
Sam (55) [Whitfield, John O.] 40
Sam [Bachlott, John Jr.] 12
Sam [Bachtoll, Alexander] 13
Sam [Banks, Dunston] 35
Sam [Bayless, Elias] 30
Sam [Bowers, William G.] 77
Sam [Cade, Guilford] 69
Sam [Dufour, Louis] 14
Sam [Harris, Jeptha V.] 37
Sam [Hartness, Robert] 38
Sam [Hester, Robert] 29, 61
Sam [Hickman, Joshua] 2
Sam [King, Harry] 15
Sam [McCartan, Thomas] 61
Sam [Palmer, Randolph] 51
Sam [Ray, Mark] 55
Sam [Robinson, Thomas] 54
Sam [Rucker, Joseph] 35
Sam [Singleton, Dr. Joseph J.] 50
Sam [Singleton, Joseph J.] 46
Sam [Smith, David John] 17
Sam [Steen, Thomas] 54
Sam [Tate, Bacon] 47
Sam [Tooke and Tooke] 63
Sam [White, Shelton] 34
Sam [Woodruff, Joseph] 5
Sam [Wyatt, William N.] 38
Sam, young [Tooke and Tooke] 63
Samuel [Key, Tandy] 50
Sandy [Crump, Robert] 29
Sandy [Fuqua, Drury B.] 22
Sandy [Newberry, Joseph C.] 16
Sapha [Tooke family] 64

Sarah (12) [McGehee, Hugh] 35
Sarah (2) [McGehee, Hugh] 35
Sarah (30) [Cade, Guilford] 69
Sarah (9) [Cade, Guilford] 69
Sarah [Bacon, Henry] 14
Sarah [Banks, Dunston] 35
Sarah [Banks, Henry] 35
Sarah [Baratte, B.] 11
Sarah [Baratte, D[?].] 12
Sarah [Barnardy, Catherine] 11
Sarah [Church, Silvanus] 15
Sarah [Clinch, D. L.] 2
Sarah [Cole, William D.] 17
Sarah [Gibson, William] 9
Sarah [Griffin, Jeremiah] 25
Sarah [Hall, Thomas] 2
Sarah [Hester, Robert] 29
Sarah [Jones, William] 20
Sarah [Kent, Peter] 74
Sarah [Lang, Richard] 9
Sarah [Lofton, James] 43
Sarah [Martin, Robert] 45
Sarah [McKindree, William] 13
Sarah [Robinson, Jane B.] 10
Sarah [Singleton, Dr. Joseph J.] 50
Sarah [Singleton, Joseph J.] 46
Sarah [Wanslow, Thomas] 33
Sarony[?] [Allen, John S.] 48
Sarrah [McLeskey, Thomas J.] 73
Sary [Gardner, Verlinda] 22
Sary [Martin, Robert] 50, 52
Sary [Oliver, Josiah] 21
Sceny [Royster, William] 41
Scilla [Pledger, James] 28
Scillar [Marks, John H.] 54
Scipio [Gibson, William] 8
Scipio [Hester, Robert] 29
Scissila [Hallum, John] 47
Scotland [Buford, William] 57
Scotland [Cannel, Tenence] 60
Scott [Grandlant, Seaton] 72
Selena [Rucker, Joseph] 34
Seller [Blakely, John] 41
Sempy [Poole, Stovall] 75
Senion [King, Henry] 64
Shade [McQueen, John] 53
Shadrach [Dowdell, James] 56
Shadrach [Taylor, James M.] 63
Shadrick [Oliver, Samuel C.] 34
Sharlott [Cole, Charles J.] 16, 18
Sharp [Hickman, Joshua] 2
Sharper [Thomas, George W.] 14
Sidney [Cargile, John R.] 55
Sie[?] [Lennard, Irbain] 65
Sigh [Hill, Abraham] 68

www.ingramcontent.com/pod-product-compliance
Lightning Source LLC
Chambersburg PA
CBHW081542040426
42448CB00015B/3195